Thomas A. Edison

and the Modernization of America

Thomas A. Edison
1847–1931

Thomas A. Edison

and the Modernization of America

Martin V. Melosi

Edited by Oscar Handlin

■ HarperCollins*Publishers*

Acknowledgment

Frontispiece photo: used with the permission of the U.S. Department of the Interior, National Park Service, Edison National Historic Site

Library of Congress Cataloging-in-Publication Data

Melosi, Martin V.
    Thomas Edison and the modernization of America / Martin V. Melosi.
        p.   cm—(The Library of American biography)
    ISBN 0-673-39625-8
    1. Edison, Thomas A. (Thomas Alva), 1847–1931. 2. Inventors—United
States—Biography. I. Title. II. Series.
TK140.E3M625   1990   621.3′092′4—dc20   89-24357
[B]   CIP

2 3 4 5 6 — RRC — 94 93 92 91 90

To Mary Ronchetto, with much affection

Editor's Preface

In the half-century after 1870, the United States reached economic maturity and soon ranked among the most advanced manufacturing societies. Historians have identified this era of rapid development as the age of trusts and robber barons who controlled large enterprises and dominated entire productive systems by mastering the channels of investment. However, trusts and robber barons played only a secondary part in the formation of a modern technological society that was dependent on the power of electricity and swift communication. Inventors, not robber barons, were at the focal points of change in this era. Inventors were not corporate types but introspective individuals who immersed themselves in their work, solved specific problems, and only later exercised the entrepreneurial skills to place their inventions in the market.

One of these individuals, Thomas A. Edison, contributed to the basic structure on which modern communications and the information age would rest. As a result of his work, the twentieth-century city ceased to depend on gas for illumination and began to move with power greater than that of the horse-car. Its residents listened to voices emanating from boxes and watched the flicker of mechanically produced images. Edison influenced the ways in which everyone worked, lived, and spent leisure time.

Edison, however, was only dimly aware of the larger significance of his endeavors. He was a problem solver, not a philosopher, and lacked a unifying conception to tie together his numorous inventions. Professor Melosi's *Thomas Edison and the Modernization of America* supplies that conception, reveals how Edison's mind worked, traces the effects of his achievements on modern life, and explains the interaction of the man and his time. For this it is especially welcome.

Oscar Handlin

Contents

Thomas A. Edison

and the Modernization of America

CHAPTER ONE

On the Urban Frontier

On April 22, 1889, President Benjamin Harrison announced the opening of the Oklahoma District to white settlement. By sunset, one hundred thousand settlers claimed more than twelve thousand homesteads, and the last major territory reserved solely for the Indians was gone. American pioneers had subdued the Great Plains.

The Superintendent of the Census marked this important moment in the history of the American West with a prophetic observation that "the unsettled areas have been so broken into by isolated bodies of settlement that there can hardly be said to be a frontier line." The closing of the frontier was echoed in "The Significance of the Frontier in American History," written by Frederick Jackson Turner in 1893. American history, he asserted, has been in large degree "the history of the colonization of the Great West. The existence of an area of free land, its continuous recession, and the advance of American settlement westward, explain American development." For the young historian from the University of Wisconsin, the frontier was the seedbed of democracy, individualism, prosperity, and inventiveness.

Although the western frontier had closed by 1900, late-nineteenth-century Americans may not have been fully aware that another had already opened in the Northeast and Midwest. The industrial city was the new frontier of business enterprise, industrial growth, social change, acquisitiveness, and technical achievement. While the western frontier faded into the nostalgic past, the industrial cities rapidly became the foremost expression of modern America.

Between 1860 and 1920 small "walking cities" became bustling industrial centers growing upward at the core and sprawling outward into the hinterland. Urban population increased more than twice as rapidly as the total United States population. In 1860 less than 20 percent of the nation's 31,000,000 people lived in cities or towns; in 1920 more than 51 percent of the almost 106,000,000 did so. There were many more cities as well; only 392 in 1860, but 2,700 in 1920—68 of which had 100,000 or more people.

The Northeast led the way in urbanizing. In the early nineteenth century, its largest cities were centers of commerce and finance. However, by mid-century urban development and industrial growth were becoming immutably linked. Within fifty years the manufacturing belt extended from Boston westward to St. Louis. Industrial cities became the centers from which economic activity, political power, and technical innovation radiated, and the expanding metropolises became the heart of a new mass culture, nurturing the growth of the modern service economy and emerging as the core of a new consumer society.

Transportation and communications were keys to growth. In 1860 the basic railroad network east of the Mississippi was complete. By 1920 the 31,000 miles of track had multiplied to more than 297,000. Four transcontinental lines pushed westward, fostering the completion of a vast urban network and helping to create a national market for a cornucopia of goods. Telegraph lines also spanned the continent, furnishing a vital communications link over thousands of miles. In fact, the transcontinental telegraph preceded the transcontinental railroad by seven years. After the Civil War, more than 200,000 miles of line were in service.

Other innovations contributed to large-scale industrialization. The steam engine liberated factories from the necessity to be near watercourses for energy needs. Factories were now able to cluster closer to a large labor force and to sources of coal and other raw materials. By the end of the century, the new factory system—dependent on power-driven machinery—mass-produced goods for the rapidly growing American population. The expansion stimulated demand for producer goods as well, including steel rails, all kinds of piping, and other construction materials.

Cities quickly became the centers of innovation and inventiveness. The urban market extended to new industries the managerial and organizational revolution that made both railroading and telegraphy big businesses. Unprecedented economic opportunity drew scientists, engineers, technicians, craftsmen, and inventors to the cities. Technical innovations enhanced existing business enterprise and created new industries. By 1910 more than one million patents had been registered with the United States Patent Office, 90 percent registered after 1870.

Thomas Alva Edison epitomized the city as the focus of innovation and invention. He presided over the modernization of America with contributions to communications, transportation, illumination, electrical power, industrial production, research and development techniques, and entrepreneurship. His hand was in every phase of the communications revolution—telegraph, telephone, radio, motion pictures, business machines, and the phonograph. His research in electricity led to the first commercial incandescent lighting system and advanced the development of the storage battery, various electric appliances, the electric streetcar, and the electric automobile. He received 1,093 patents. His Menlo Park and West Orange laboratories pioneered the idea of integrated research facilities. And the dozens of companies he spawned—including General Electric and Thomas A. Edison, Inc.—were important parts of the organizational revolution in business.

Thomas Edison's life (1847–1931) spanned the period when the United States shifted from a burgeoning industrial society to a consumer-oriented, city-dominated mass culture. His inventions and his wide-ranging interests spoke to the wants of that new culture. In addition, he helped establish the technical and commercial structure central to modern America. He became a professional inventor and businessman operating in and for a modern urban society. From his boyhood encounters in Detroit to the establishment of his research laboratories and industrial plants in New York and New Jersey, Edison and the city were inseparable.

Before his trek to the big city, however, Thomas Edison's nurturing took place in small towns on the old frontier. Records of his ancestry and childhood are sparse, but enough remains to provide clues to the circumstances of his upbringing, the opportunities he had, and the kind of adult he was to become.

The Edison family was part Dutch and part English, although the origins of the family in Europe are uncertain. They were sturdy pioneering stock, often long-lived, and staunchly individualistic. What they lacked in education, they made up in strongly held opinions.

John Edison—Thomas Edison's great-grandfather—was the first of the family line in America. In 1765 he married Sarah Ogden, who came from a well-known landed family in New Jersey. John subsequently became proprietor of a seventy-five-acre farm in the township of Caldwell, Essex County, New Jersey. His good fortune turned sour in 1776 when he lost his farm to confiscation as a result of Tory leanings during the American Revolution and was forced to seek safe haven in New York. He returned to New Jersey to fight against the revolutionary forces but was captured and sentenced to death for treason. Fortunately, through the influence of the Ogden family, he was spared.

The Edisons emigrated to Canada in 1783, and after several months of waiting, were given a grant of land in Nova Scotia because of their devotion to the mother country. Their new property was near Digby in a desolate spot along the east coast of the Bay of Fundy. Making the most of their situation, the family worked hard to rebuild what they had lost in New Jersey.

For twenty-eight years the Edisons worked their land in the foggy wilderness of Nova Scotia. But in 1811, with the family growing too large to eke out a living, they decided to move westward. They were drawn to Ontario Province, where they received several hundred acres of pineland along the Otter

River, which was two miles inland from Lake Erie between Toronto and Detroit. Again they carved out a home in the wilderness, but they found Ontario to be a more hospitable environment than Nova Scotia.

No sooner had they arrived in Ontario than the War of 1812 broke out. Samuel Ogden, the eldest of John and Sarah's children (and Thomas Edison's grandfather), shared his father's loyalty to King and County and fought against the Americans. Captain Samuel also carried on the tradition of raising a large family—a precedent well set by his father. He had eight children by his first wife Nancy. At almost sixty he became a widower, married again, and had five more children.

By the time Sam had remarried in 1825, the Edison settlement had become a village and took the name, Vienna. The numerous Edison boys worked at lumbering and carpentry as well as on the farm. Samuel Ogden, Jr., who would become Thomas Edison's father, was Sam, Sr.'s sixth child. He was born in Digby in 1804, and was twenty-one when his father started his second family. He had tried several trades, but was best known as a tavernkeeper in Vienna.

In 1828 Sam, Jr., married Nancy Elliott, who was a teacher in a recently established two-room school in Vienna. Nancy was born in 1810 in New York, where her father, Reverend John Elliott, was a Baptist minister. The family moved from New Berlin in Chenango County, New York, to Vienna to preach in the local Baptist church. Sam, Jr., and Nancy had four children while living in Canada—Marion (1829), William Pitt (1831), Harriet Ann (1833), and Carlile (1836).

Sam, Jr., was tall and strong with a fiery temper. He was characteristically independent for an Edison, with a rebellious nature and a free-thinking spirit. Despite his Tory heritage, he was strongly influenced by the writings of revolutionary stalwart Thomas Paine and complained often about the limits to representative government in Ontario. It was not uncommon for local agitators to gather at his tavern to debate the political issues of the time.

In the 1830s an insurrection in Ontario led by William Lyon Mackenzie was afoot, and Sam, Jr., was identified as a leader. In

December 1837 Mackenzie and a few hundred rebels made a desperate bid for power, but were routed and were forced to flee. Sam, Jr., and some other rebels were marching on Toronto when news of the fiasco reached him. With soldiers rapidly approaching, he decided to escape alone across the border to the United States. Since he was soon indicted for treason, he had little choice but to remain.

Sam, Jr., moved his family to Milan, Ohio, in 1839, where he hoped to make a new start. Situated eight miles south of Lake Erie on the Huron River, Milan occupied the site of an old Indian village that once contained a Moravian mission. The timing of their move was propitious, because in that year the town celebrated the opening of a three-mile canal that connected it to a navigable portion of the river. In the 1840s Milan became an important grain depot and a prosperous shipbuilding and regional manufacturing center.

Sam prospered in this new environment. Among other things, he speculated in land and established a lumber business that supplied shingles and timber for the town. He also built a substantial wood-frame and brick house for his family. By 1847 three more children had been added to the Edison family—Samuel O. (1840), Eliza (1844), and Thomas Alva (1847). Unfortunately, only four reached adulthood: Carlile, Samuel O., and Eliza did not survive beyond childhood.

The youngest Edison, Thomas Alva, was born on February 11, 1847. The United States was then rounding out its continental empire, pushing the borders to the Pacific Coast and the Gulf of Mexico. During that same year Brigham Young's first band of Mormons reached the Great Salt Lake. Texas, Oregon Territory, California, and much of the Southwest all became part of the United States. Young Edison had a first-hand view of the relentless push to the Pacific. As a three-year-old he saw prairie schooners parked in the town streets, a stop on their way to the California gold fields. This was an early memory he never forgot.

He was named "Thomas" after Sam's older brother, who also lived in Milan, and "Alva" after Captain Alva Bradley, a master of ships on Lake Erie and one of Sam's friends. Many years after his birth a bizarre story circulated that Thomas Edison was actually of Mexican ancestry. One version of the story suggested that Tomas de Alva was a very poor Mexican orphan who roamed the streets of El Paso, Texas, until he was subsequently adopted by a well-to-do American named Edison. Such was the eventual celebrity of the inventor that many countries longed to claim him or his accomplishments.

During his childhood, Thomas Edison was known as "Al." His twenty-year-old sister, Marion, and his sixteen-year-old sister, Harriet Ann—nicknamed Tannie—looked after him when he was very young. When Marion got married in 1849, Al was heartbroken. Only Tannie lived at home with her brother on a regular basis, since Pitt was often away on business. However, Al had playmates, nearby relatives, and occasional boarders to amuse him.

Because Al was sickly—and because Nancy had already lost some of her children—his mother lavished attention on her youngest, fussing over him and treating him much like an only child. Young Al's childhood, however, was hardly unusual or extraordinary. He got into the typical scrapes that befell young boys, and he showed a not-so-atypical lack of interest in school. Sometimes when he was left to play alone, his curiosity got him into trouble. He fell into the pit of a grain elevator and almost suffocated, and he allegedly started a fire in his father's shed, which—as the story goes—earned him a whipping in the town square. However, there is little evidence that such a public event took place. Sometimes his curiosity simply led him to harmless leaps of logic. For example, after questioning his mother about how geese hatch their eggs, he patiently sat atop an egg in a neighbor's barn waiting for the blessed event.

One somber note was the drowning of one of Al's playmates, a son of Milan's most prominent storekeeper. The boys were swimming in a stream near the Edison house when the boy disappeared under the water. Perplexed and uncertain, the six-year-old returned home. What went on in his mind at the time is impossible to say, but Edison never forgot the incident.

The event that most significantly altered Al's childhood was the changing economic fortunes of Milan. The Columbus,

Sandusky, and Hocking Railroad from the lake port of San-dusky to Columbus and Hockingport on the Ohio, bypassed Milan thus capturing much of the canal's traffic. As Milan's boom peaked, so did Sam Edison's opportunities. In the spring of 1854 the family moved to Port Huron, Michigan, a flourishing lumber town sixty miles northeast of Detroit. Although an iso-lated spot on the Canadian border, Port Huron with a popula-tion of 3,100 was twice the size of Milan.

Sam hoped to make his fortune from the opportunity that Michigan offered. Although his listed occupation was "farmer," he revelled in land speculation and took up lumbering again. One curious enterprise was building a hundred-foot wooden observation tower overlooking Lake Huron and the St. Clair River, a sure-fire tourist attraction.

The family owned a spacious two-story, six-bedroom house—more than adequate for the Edisons with only Pitt, Tan-nie, and Al living at home. By the time Al was nine, both Tannie and Pitt were married, leaving him the only child to care for. Since the Edisons lived outside of town and were separated from most of their family, Nancy devoted much of her time to educating her son. In fact, Al received much of his basic educa-tion at home, where Nancy organized lessons and prepared an extensive reading program. He was encouraged to master the home library and particularly relished reading popular science periodicals and contemporary fiction. He even received a healthy dose of his father's devotion to Thomas Paine.

Al briefly attended the private school of Reverend G.B. Engle. However, he responded poorly to the rote teaching methods and the regimented atmosphere of the school. The Reverend and his wife took Al's unattentiveness as a sign that he was a problem child. Some thought he was "a little addled," his father confessed. But Nancy knew this was not true. Her teaching experience combined with her motherly instincts made her a more patient teacher than Engle. Al's response was utter devotion to her. Years later he noted, "My mother was the making of me. She was so true, so sure of me, and I felt I had some one to live for, some one I must not disappoint."

The Edisons did not give up totally on formal education for their son. Al briefly attended the local public school in Port Huron and sometimes frequented Sunday school. But his innate curiosity, his need to experiment, and his solid training at home made Al tepid about the value of formal education. He later noted that it cast "the brain into a mould" and "[did] not encourage original thought or reasoning," laying "more stress on memory than on observation."

Edison's eye for the practical, the tangible, the mundane, and the material left him traits he nurtured throughout his life. Reading was his favorite entertainment, and he delighted in books that dealt with mechanical things or told interesting stories. He was fascinated with machinery and purportedly built a miniature steam-powered sawmill and railroad. He also tried scores of chemical experiments. Sometimes he took his experimenting too far, as in talking his friend Michael Oates into drinking Seidlitz powder. He wanted to see if the resulting gas would make Oates fly. All it did was to make the boy nauseous. While Al lacked the patience to sit in a classroom and be talked at, he quickly demonstrated the intellectual tenacity to experiment—even if it got him the switch, as in the case of Michael Oates.

Formal education for youths of Al's social and economic status rarely extended beyond the sixth grade. When Al took a job on the Grand Trunk Railroad at age twelve, he was hardly a deviant or misfit. More important in Edison's life than formal schooling was the railroad, which made him more financially independent, gave him practical business experience, and brought him into contact with many types of people. The railroad introduced him to city life in Detroit, nurtured his interest in telegraphy, and moved him to adulthood.

The railroad undermined the economic fortunes of Milan; in Port Huron it offered young Edison opportunity. In November 1859 the Grand Trunk Railroad crossed from Canada into Michigan, opening a branch line from Detroit to Fort Gratiot, within walking distance of the Edison home. Al was fascinated with steam locomotives and jumped at a job as "candy butcher" on the Grand Trunk Railroad, where he sold newspapers, magazines, candies, and tobacco on the train to Detroit. Eventually, the conductor gave him permission to store dairy products and fresh produce in the baggage car—goods he hawked along the route. He readily took to sales and to this budding entrepreneurship.

The hours were long—he left Port Huron at 7:15 A.M. and returned home at 8:00 P.M.—but he had plenty of time along the route to pursue a number of interests. After he sold his candies, papers, and produce, his time was his own. He set up a chemical laboratory in the baggage car and passed many hours carrying out experiments. He also set up a printing press. In 1862 he began the *Grand Trunk Herald*, which carried news from along the railroad line. After a celebrated phosphorous fire on the train, the irate conductor forced Edison to dispose of the lab and the printing press, but he at least retained his job. Immediately after the *Herald*, he developed a partnership with a printer named William Wright and published *Paul Pry*, which was based in Port Huron and was a little more sensationalistic and gossipy.

Edison was getting a taste of entrepreneurship, which must have made his father proud. Off the train, he set up stands in Port Huron to sell produce purchased in Detroit and newspapers and magazines. His only setback was his noticeable loss of hearing, which grew worse in later life. Popular lore dates the beginnings of his deafness to the phosphorus fire in the baggage car when the train conductor allegedly boxed his ear. Edison himself stated that "the injury that permanently deafened me was caused by my being lifted by the ears from where I stood upon the ground into the baggage car." More likely, it had come on gradually due to his chronic illnesses as a small child.

Edison's access to Detroit pointed the way to his future. The oldest city in the Midwest, Detroit began as a fortified French outpost in 1701. The coming of the railroad, the opening of the Soo Canals in 1855, and the subsequent development of industry resulted in a city of 45,600 by 1860. Detroit offered experiences and opportunities that a young man was not likely to find in small-town Ohio or Michigan. Since chemicals and pharmaceuticals were among the city's principal products, Al had ready access to unending supplies for his laboratory. He spent a great deal of time in the reading room of the Young Men's Association—soon reorganized as the Detroit Free Library. In later life he boasted that "I didn't read a few books. I read the library." While this was an exaggeration, he nonetheless worked his way through a wide variety of literature, dime novels, and some technical books.

Detroit also introduced him to a wider variety of people. In the railroad yard he talked to the switchmen. He met telegraphers and men in machine shops. "The happiest time of my life was when I was twelve years old," he later recalled. "I was just old enough to have a good time in the world, but not old enough to understand any of its troubles." The railroad and Detroit propelled him toward his future as a professional inventor and businessman in the modern American city. Al was not to remain a smalltown boy for long. He was self-trained and self-made in a world where that was still possible. The Midwestern cities began to offer Edison evidence of the new industrial age, to fire his curiosity and his ambitions.

CHAPTER TWO

Itinerant Telegrapher

"Well, we are a severed nation. We are a divided house. And we are none the worse for it," stated an editorial in the *Indianapolis Daily Journal* in response to the secession of South Carolina from the Union in December 1860. "We are well rid of South Carolina," it added, "if we are only wise enough to count it a riddance, and nothing worse . . ."

This flip, if indignant, reaction did not anticipate the crisis that would befall the United States during the five years to follow. Between January 9 and February 1, 1861, six states joined South Carolina in rebellion—Mississippi, Florida, Alabama, Georgia, Louisiana, and Texas. On April 12, South Carolina ordered Major Robert Anderson at the federal installation at Fort Sumter to surrender immediately. When he refused, shore batteries from Charleston fired on the fort, and on the next day Anderson surrendered. The Civil War had begun.

By the end of May, Virginia, Arkansas, Tennessee, and North Carolina also had joined the Confederate States of America. Both Union and Confederacy accused the other of provoking the conflict. Nearly one million Americans died by the end of the hostilities in 1865 in the bloodiest war in the nation's history. In the aftermath, the lives of countless people changed— black freedmen, the families of fallen soldiers, veterans, Southern planters, political leaders—and the consequences shaped the political and social future of the United States for generations.

Thomas Edison was fourteen in 1861, too young to fight. But he was old enough to follow the war's progress and to exploit it for his own ends. As an incipient businessman, Edison saw an opportunity to tap the war's newsworthiness while remaining far from the battlelines. "I decided," he later recalled, "that if I could send ahead to outlying stations a hint of the big war news which, I, there in Detroit had learned was coming, I could do better than normal business when I reached them."

On April 6, 1862, the day of the famous Confederate surprise attack at Shiloh Church, Edison unwrapped his money-making scheme. He bargained with a friendly telegrapher on the Grand Trunk in Detroit to wire a bulletin about the bloody encounter to the stations along the line. And he acquired one thousand newspapers on consignment, instead of his usual one hundred. At every station, Al Edison found the eager crowds he had hoped for and sold his papers at inflated prices. By the end of the day, he had made a tidy sum of money and had earned a reputation as a hustler.

The Civil War launched Edison's career as a telegrapher. The years of war constituted his passage to adulthood, began his apprenticeship as an inventor, and also taught him to live and work away from home, as he wandered from one job to the other in the major cities of the Midwest and Upper South. The life of the itinerant operator, while hardly glamorous, fulfilled adolescent wanderlust and suited his independent nature. As a telegrapher, he had a job with limited supervision, clearly defined responsibilities, and tangible results. He also had time on his hands to pursue his experiments and his reading. As a relatively new commercial venture and as an innovative technology, telegraphy focused Edison's scientific curiosity and opened the door to much broader inquiries into electricity and electromagnetism.

In 1837 William F. Cooke and Charles Wheatstone completed a working telegraph line in England. Seven years later Samuel F. B. Morse and Alfred Vail successfully communicated their famous message, "What hath God wrought," on an experimental line from Washington, D.C., to Baltimore. Congress had appropriated thirty thousand dollars to build the line, and in 1845 the Post Office assumed operation, employing Morse as superintendent. In the following year, however, financial and management problems forced the Post Office to turn over the line to private development.

Very rapidly a number of small companies competed to wire the nation. Within two years of the Morse-Vail demonstration, telegraph promoter Henry O'Reilly extended a line to Philadelphia. A New York-to-Philadelphia line completed by Morse and associates then linked Washington to New York. By 1851 eleven lines spread out from the great port city. In addition, others extended westward to Pittsburgh, Cincinnati, and Louisville. Every state east of the Mississippi, except Florida, was connected to the telegraphic network by 1848. In December of that year, telegraph lines carried President James K. Polk's message to Congress as far west as St. Louis, where newspapers printed it within twenty-four hours. The telegraph reached California by 1861, linking the far-flung states of the young nation. By the eve of the Civil War, the United States boasted more than fifty thousand miles of wire serving more than eight hundred places.

Despite impulsive construction practices and the gargantuan task of devising a new communications network for a whole continent, the telegraph quickly became an essential feature of American life. The most dramatic impact was on news gathering, social communications, and commercial life. Within two weeks of the stringing of the Washington–Baltimore line, the telegraph demonstrated its value by carrying news of the Democratic National Convention. It flashed accounts of the war with Mexico and the Civil War to a nation hungry for news of the fighting. The telegraph vastly improved the ability to relay information from the war front to the newspapers, and it kept military commanders in close contact with their units. During the Civil War alone, telegraphers transmitted more than six million messages.

Transcontinental telegraphy preceded transcontinental railroad track, helping to connect western farms, ranches, and mines with eastern markets. Telegraph companies used railroad routes for their rights-of-way, and in turn the railroads used telegraphic communications to manage their systems. Railroad officials also relied upon the telegraph to control traffic along crowded trunk lines in the East. After the Civil War, many of the telegraph companies became subsidiaries of railroads.

The practical application of the telegraph led to the first international communications system. The transatlantic cable was a costly and audacious venture, developed and financed by the British, who also pioneered much of the technology for submarine telegraphy. Cooperation on the American side came from Cyrus W. Field, a wealthy paper manufacturer from Massachusetts. After several failures, the cable was successfully laid in July 1866. The telegraph, at home and abroad, had conquered distance and time.

By mid-century, the vital communications and transportation networks spawned new commercial and industrial activity by providing fast and dependable service essential to high-volume production and distribution. Equally important, the rail and telegraph companies were the first modern business enterprises in the United States. They required large numbers of full-time managers and sophisticated new administrative systems.

Dozens of new telegraph companies sprung up all over the country in the 1850s. Until the 1860s they were essentially local or regional operations interconnecting a few cities at most. Three regional companies, however, operated the network by the end of the Civil War: Western Union, the American Telegraph Company, and the United States Telegraph Company. Of them, Western Union benefitted the most from the war as a result of substantial government subsidies and because its lines, which ran primarily east to west, remained intact. With forty-four thousand miles of telegraph line, Western Union had more than the combined total of its two major competitors.

As telegraph traffic declined after the war, Western Union engaged in price wars to cripple its competitors. In 1866 it absorbed American Telegraph and United States Telegraph and thus dominated the industry. Although more than two hundred companies remained in existence, all but four were tiny. Nevertheless, independent regional companies and new companies persisted in challenging Western Union on its most profitable routes. The telephone did not rival the telegraph until the end of the nineteenth century.

Intense interest in science, his relentless tinkering with machinery, and his work on the Grand Trunk drew Thomas Edison to telegraphy in the 1860s. He coaxed telegraph operators at the depots to give him some basic instruction, and he and a friend strung a line between their houses to practice. Too independent and undisciplined to hold down a routine job with strict supervision, he reveled in the life of the tramp telegrapher. In addition, the Civil War created the opportunity for Edison to pursue his interest because most of the experienced telegraphers had rushed into the Military Telegraph Corps or had enlisted in the army.

After accumulating a windfall as a result of his exploitation of Shiloh, Al Edison was bent on becoming a telegraph operator. "You can understand why it struck me then," he later recalled, "that the telegraph must be about the best thing going, for it was the telegraphic notices on the bulletin boards which had done the trick. I determined at once to become a telegraph operator."

His chance came on the Mt. Clemens platform in August 1862. Three-year-old Jimmy Mackenzie was playing in the gravel on the main track when a heavy boxcar shunted out of a siding and began rolling toward him. Al Edison threw "his papers . . . upon the platform with his . . . cap, and plunged to the rescue, risking his own life to save his little friend, and throwing the child and himself out of the way. . . ." James U. Mackenzie, the anxious father, was grateful for Edison's heroic act. To return the favor, Mackenzie offered to teach Al Edison railroad telegraphy. The young man jumped at the opportunity.

Mackenzie, a twenty-five-year-old red-haired Scotsman, was station agent at Mt. Clemens. He had been a telegrapher at Point Edward, just across the river from Port Huron, and had supplied Al with telegraph news for the *Grand Trunk Herald*'s "Hot Off the Wires" column. At the time of the rescue,

Mackenzie was training another apprentice, but he took on young Edison as well for a couple of months in August or September 1862. Edison had already built his own crude telegraphic instrument and learned Morse Code.

While the commercial application of the telegraph was a major undertaking, the system of telegraphy that Edison learned was relatively simple. The basic components included a transmitting key, an electromagnetic relay for receiving electrical impulses, and a register for recording the messages on paper tape. In the 1850s, most registers were replaced by "sounders," which turned electric impulses into clicks of a lever against a sounding piece. Since the telegraph only required low voltage to operate, current from a battery was sufficient. Messages were sent by code, consisting of dots and dashes—long and short electrical impulses—that represented letters of the alphabet.

Despite the demand for telegraphers, Al Edison needed seasoning before he could compete effectively for first-class jobs. By the winter of 1862 he had progressed sufficiently to get a position as Western Union telegraph operator for Port Huron. The office—just a small table—was located in Micah Walker's jewelry store. Al Edison earned less than one-quarter the amount a journeyman telegrapher commanded—about twenty to twenty-five dollars a month. However, he had a chance to practice his new craft, and he had ample time to conduct chemical and electrical experiments and to read *Scientific American*. Al was hardly the ideal employee, however, transmitting messages poorly and receiving them with below-average skill. Much to Mr. Walker's consternation, he devoted too much time to his own experiments, sometimes damaging the fine watchmaking instruments by using them for other than delicate repairs. At fifteen, Edison had yet to exhibit much responsibility.

But ready or not, he took up the life of a tramp telegrapher between 1863 and 1867. When Walker tried to apprentice Al for twenty dollars a month, Sam Edison would not let his son accept. Al then applied for a job as a railway telegraph operator on the Grand Trunk line. Through friend Mackenzie's help, he secured a night job at Stratford Junction, Ontario, in Bayham township. He received twenty-five dollars a month.

The job was not demanding, and while Edison enjoyed the work, the long quiet periods gave him time to read and work on research projects. His priorities got easily confused. For example, between the hours of 9:00 P.M. and 7:00 A.M., operators were required to send the signal "6" to the train dispatcher's office each hour to insure that they were alert. In order to take short naps while on duty, Edison constructed a small wheel with notches on the rim and attached it to a clock. Each hour the wheel revolved and at the proper time sent the "sixing" message automatically. The supervisor was not amused. After detecting the mechanism, he reprimanded Edison.

A more serious breach sometime later cost him his job. One evening a train ran past the station before he could hold it. While an accident was avoided, this proved to be too close a call. General Manager W. J. Spicer was furious and threatened to have Edison and his supervisor shipped off to jail. Fortunately, the general manager was temporarily distracted, and Edison bolted, hopping a train for Sarnia. Thus began what was a typical life for a tramp telegrapher—little job security and constant relocation. Young Edison brought on some of his bad luck himself; few of his moves occurred because he was naturally restless. His preoccupation with his experiments and his reading often did him in. On the other hand, he was beginning to show the glimmer of his talents as an inventor with his imaginative alarm device.

After Stratford Junction, he returned to Port Huron. In early 1864 he landed a job with the Lake Shore and Michigan Southern Railroad near Adrian, sixty miles southwest of Detroit. This was another "night trick," which he enjoyed, but once again misfortune loomed. Ordered by his supervisor to break in on a line to send an important dispatch, he did so against the protest of the receiver on the other end. Unfortunately the receiver was the superintendent, and Edison was promptly fired. A short two-month stint followed in Fort Wayne, Indiana. What glamour Edison had associated with the life of the itinerant telegrapher was quickly dimming.

Edison was not the usual tramp telegrapher, however. Whether he realized it or not, the job—as he practiced it—was a training ground for work in an industry where technical changes were rapid and business opportunities abounded. The men who made their living as tramp telegraphers were a rare breed. They were often splendid operators but incredibly undisciplined and with few ambitions. Normally well paid, but subject to nervous tension brought on by the rigors of sending and receiving messages, they often found relief in a bottle. Edison, by contrast, began as a marginal telegrapher. Although he improved his skills in time, he was more often preoccupied with tinkering and experiments than with his assigned tasks.

Telegraphy was, among other things, a training ground for the newly emerging field of electrical engineering. Some men who began as operators turned to maintaining and improving the system. In time a class of telegraphic workers, called "electricians," emerged. Their job was to maintain the lines and to keep the transmitting and receiving apparatus in working order. These men became the engineers of the industry at a time when there were no formally trained electrical engineers. In fact, not until the American Electrical Society—founded in Chicago in the mid-1870s—was there an organization to tout their professional status.

Edison, however, was part of a smaller group of former operators who used their experience to make a mark in invention and entrepreneurship. They aspired to be more than technicians, more than technical advisers or consultants to management. Telegraphy for them was a springboard into other ventures, and it offered Edison some valuable experiences that he retained throughout his life.

In 1864 Edison headed for Indianapolis, which was a major rail shipping center in the 1860s, boasting more than one hundred manufacturing and industrial companies. He found a job on the payroll of Western Union as a plug—or second-class—operator at the busy Union Depot, which served as a junction for all the rail lines in the area. His duty was on the "way wire" linking small towns in the telegraph system.

While thus employed, Edison produced what he later called his first invention—a Morse repeater. After frustrating experiences trying to keep up with the fast pace of the press wire, he arranged two old Morse embossing registers to slow the presentation of messages. One register recorded the incoming signal, while the other played it back at a slower speed. Edison and E. L. Parmelee, a fellow operator, used the repeater to receive press reports. Although the principle was sound, the newspapers complained about receiving uneven copy and the practice ceased. However, the two operators adjusted the registers to repeat messages from one circuit to another and tested them on a Pittsburgh-to-St. Louis line.

Whether the repeater can actually be considered Edison's first invention is open to conjecture. The alarm he built at Stratford Junction was certainly a device made by original effort. But there is little doubt—no matter what is labeled as his first invention—that Edison was beginning to consider himself as more than an operator. He not only learned the basic mechanical and electrical operation of the telegraph system but pored over literature and tried to broaden his understanding of the scientific principles underlying the technology. And as his expertise grew, he began keeping notebooks with comments and drawings gleaned from his readings and his own experiments. He was rapidly becoming one in a line of inventors who sought to enhance the speed, accuracy, and utility of the telegraph.

Young men like Edison saw opportunities in the shortcomings of the new communications system. And shortcomings there were. By the time of the Civil War, several problems were still unresolved. Noninsulated wires and poor line-stringing practices made the system vulnerable to changing weather conditions. Sending messages over long distances was difficult. Messages could not be sent more than two hundred miles without being taken off the wire and retransmitted. For example, to send a message from Boston to St. Louis required six such transfers. And sending and receiving more than one message at a time over a single wire was experimentally possible but had not been practically or commercially introduced.

In spring 1865 Edison left Indianapolis for Cincinnati because it provided him a better opportunity as an inventor. He heard about the opening from Ezra Gilliland, an acquaintance from Adrian who worked with him on the night shift at the Western Union office. By the time he settled in Cincinnati, he was still much the country hick that his colleagues took him for. However, his association with Gilliland and Nat Hyams, a comedian working at a local stage, expanded his social life. He attended the theater more often and briefly contemplated becoming an actor. His tastes in reading broadened. But the most significant change was in his maturation in the telegraphy field. He rose from plug to a first-class operator, and the additional money (one hundred twenty-five dollars a month) allowed him to expand his experiments. He became increasingly interested in developing a duplex telegraph—to send two messages simultaneously over the same wire—and made some preliminary sketches.

Cincinnati also gave him greater exposure to big-city life. From the vantage point of his job, Cincinnati was an important telegraph center. Many bright young men had parlayed experience as operators there into better positions with more responsibility and more money. The big cities, especially, benefitted from the spreading telegraph system. Urban merchants and manufacturers gained great advantage in information gathering and capital accumulation because they dominated telegraph usage through mid-century. Telegraph companies also tended to give wire-access preference to "through business" between major cities over "way business" involving places smaller in population and with less economic importance.

Cincinnati, the commercial center of the Ohio River valley, was the biggest city young Edison had ever lived in. By 1862 it had become the pork packing center of the United States and also specialized in related industries such as soap and oil production and leather making. William Procter and James Gamble were among its best-known business leaders. Their company reportedly paid Edison to install a private-line telegraph while he lived there.

The railroad and the telegraph had accelerated the growth of Midwestern cities, linking them into a national network. The new transportation and communications systems helped to open new territory for agricultural development, thus creating vast new markets and intensifying demand for consumer goods. The Civil War did not end the momentum of city-building in the Midwest. Interior river commerce deteriorated, but the railroad and rising patterns of east-west trade sustained cities such as Cincinnati, Chicago, and St. Louis. What began as commercial hubs in the early nineteenth century emerged as industrial centers soon after the war. In 1860 Cincinnati was the seventh largest city (161,044) in the country, St. Louis was eighth (160,773), Chicago ninth (109,260), Louisville twelfth (68,033), Pittsburgh seventeenth (49,221), Detroit nineteenth (45,619), and Cleveland twenty-first (43,417). For a young man on the rise, the city was the place to be.

While in Cincinnati, Edison matured as a telegraph operator. On September 17, 1865, he and his fellow telegraphers established a local chapter of the National Telegraphic Union and went off to celebrate. Edison, who was not much of a drinker, declined. That night the operators failed to make the evening shift, and Edison recorded the incoming press reports himself. His skills had improved noticeably, and the copy met the newspapers' needs. Office manager J. F. Stevens was so impressed with this show of responsibility that he promoted Edison to operator first-class.

Soon after his promotion, Edison moved to Memphis. A major commercial city on the Mississippi, Memphis served as Confederate capital of Tennessee until 1862, when it was captured by federal gunboats. When the eighteen-year-old operator first-class arrived, the city had returned to civilian control but was lawless and raucous. Despite the confusion, he immersed himself in work, taking a job as a press-wire operator and reading voraciously. He even began learning Spanish, French, and Latin. He conducted several experiments on repeaters, claiming to have hooked up New Orleans to New York with a direct line for the first time since the end of the war. He also worked on duplex systems, which permitted sending two messages on the same wire simultaneously. But again, his ceaseless experimenting got him into trouble with his supervisor, and he was fired.

After Memphis Edison drifted to Louisville, an industrial center on the Ohio River, which served as a supply depot for

Union troops during the war. He worked a press wire for Western Union for a time but impulsively left Louisville in July 1866 to seek a job as a telegrapher in Brazil with two friends. The timing was not good for this adventure and terminated in New Orleans. The race riot that took place days before their arrival resulted in the commandeering under martial law of the steamship they planned to take to Brazil. Edison briefly returned to Port Huron, and then made his way back to Louisville.

In Louisville he went to work for Western Union again and continued his reading and his experimenting. The job helped to refine his telegraphic skills but resulted in another sacking—this time for spilling sulfuric acid that leaked through the floor into the manager's office below. He then returned to Cincinnati and began to delve even more deeply into his experiments and to improve his technical competence. Charles Summers, superintendent of telegraphs for the Indianapolis, Cincinnati, and Lafayette Railroad, encouraged him to continue his inventing. They worked together on a self-adjusting relay, and Edison set up a small room with tools to carry out some of his work. At the urging of another telegrapher, Edison also began developing a secret signaling system which he hoped to sell to the government.

Edison left Cincinnati in October 1867 and returned home to Michigan. The family had suffered some economic setbacks, were forced out of the Port Huron home, and had moved into another house at Fort Gratiot. Sam did not have the farm any longer but continued to speculate in land and became a justice of the peace. Bent on continuing his own work, however, Al Edison spent his six-month stay at home designing telegraph apparatus.

His years adrift in Midwestern cities moved him closer, albeit through a circuitous route, to a career as a professional inventor. His wanderings would cease as he focused his talents even more sharply on producing a host of inventions for a modernizing urban society. He also would begin to appreciate the linkages among investment, research, invention, and the marketplace. His life would become much more interesting, but infinitely more complicated.

CHAPTER THREE

An Inventor's Apprenticeship

❖
❖

In 1869 the world shrank. The Suez Canal, opened on November 17, revolutionizing oceanic transport. Before that time, a ship departing London for Ceylon—off the southern tip of India—had to travel more than twelve thousand statute miles via Cape Town. With the new canal, that same ship traveled less than eight thousand statute miles by means of a passage cut through Egypt between the Mediterranean Sea and the Red Sea. The canal recast the economy of the region and drastically altered commercial routes. At the same time, it heightened the rivalry between the colonial powers—France and England—and virtually made Egypt a financial vassal of Europe.

As the Old World grew smaller but more complex in 1869, the United States was experiencing a similar transformation. On May 10, a golden spike and a champagne toast commemorated the linking of the Union Pacific Railroad and the Central Pacific Railroad at Promontory Point, Utah, near the northern tip of the Great Salt Lake. The nation's first transcontinental railroad was complete.

The transcontinental line, negotiated by aggressive business leaders, financed by a massive federal commitment of public lands, and built by thousands of overburdened but tenacious laborers, was an event of major proportions. It opened the West to further growth, joining the remnants of the American frontier to the industrializing and urbanizing East. Western merchants were dependent on eastern markets. Western farmers sought equipment manufactured in the East or imported from Europe. Frontier colonies, which absorbed thousands of new settlers, increasingly demanded eastern goods and craved eastern styles. And more than before, the federal government's presence was felt in the West, with countless post offices, assay offices, military outposts, land offices, and train stations.

Significantly, telegraph operators first flashed the news of the last spike at Promontory Point both to the East and to the West, since the national hookup preceded the railroad line by eight years. The contribution of the telegraph to spanning the distances of the vast North American continent was matched by its role in transforming intra-urban communications. Thomas Edison's career as an inventor began as the new innovations in transportation and communication were shrinking the world in the late nineteenth century. His own work in telegraphy contributed directly to the communication revolution, and to the new era of experimentation with electricity which was to follow.

By the 1860s the railroad industry was already dominated by big business, but communications technology and the marketing of the urban telegraph had yet to become firmly established. An enterprising inventor had opportunities in such a field. Yet Edison was soon forced to realize that becoming an inventor in a world of corporations required more than perseverance or creative genius. Financing, marketing, and manufacturing were essential adjuncts to invention, and often demanded as much imagination as the creative process. Invention also required, in many cases, uneasy partnerships in the marketplace. To succeed amidst cutthroat competition and rigorous patent battles the inventor needed to ally himself with an astute businessman, or become an entrepreneur himself.

In the spring of 1868, with the help of his friend Milt Adams, the twenty-one-year-old Edison landed a job in the Boston Western Union office. The move to Boston gave him the opportunity to make the transition from telegraph operator to professional inventor. An article in the June 1868 issue of the *Journal of the Telegraph* carried an article on "Mr. Thomas A. Edison, of the Western Union Office, Boston," which mentioned his invention of a "mode of transmission both ways on a single wire . . . which is interesting, simple and ingenious."

This overly optimistic announcement about the "multiplex" telegraph was signed by Adams but written under Edison's supervision. Edison's intention to turn to full-time inventing was obvious. He thrived in the Boston environment, broadening his understanding of telegraphy through more voracious reading of technical journals and through his own experiments. In a local bookshop, he purchased Michael Faraday's *Experimental Researches in Electricity*. He had seen the volumes earlier in the Cincinnati Free Library, and reading them reinforced Edison's belief that experimentation was the key to knowledge. "I think I must have tried about everything in those books," Edison recalled. "[Faraday's] explanations were simple. He used no mathematics. He was the Master Experimenter."

A brief notice in the January 1869 issue of *The Telegrapher*, a small trade journal, reported that Edison had resigned his job at the Western Union office and would "hereafter devote his full time to bringing out his inventions." With youthful enthusiasm and astonishing self-confidence, Edison abandoned the certainty of a paycheck for more lofty ambitions.

Boston was an ideal place from which to launch a career as an inventor. With a population of more than two hundred thousand, it was the fifth largest city in the country and the heart of New England. An influential commercial and industrial seaport, it was also a major center of intellectual life, boasting Harvard and the Massachusetts Institute of Technology just across the Charles River in Cambridge.

Boston was the hub of scientific and electrical research in the United States, abounding with scientists, technicians, skilled artisans, and tinkerers of all types. This formidable city was the home of Samuel Morse and Charles Williams, Jr.—a leading telegraph manufacturer—whose factory on Court Street was a haven for experimenters. Alexander Graham Bell worked on his early telephone at Williams's shop, as did Moses G. Farmer, the most prominent American electrical inventor of his day. Thomas Hall, who produced a miniature electric-motored train, and Joseph B. Stearns, president of Franklin Telegraph Company and inventor of a duplex telegraph system, were occupants of the same building.

No sooner had Edison arrived in Boston than he discovered the Court Street factory. It was the young inventor's equivalent of the neighborhood pool hall or barber shop. He bought equipment there for his own experiments and exchanged ideas with others. He produced an operating model of his first patented invention, the vote recorder, at Court Street.

The telegraph and its communications offshoots were the focal point of electrical invention. By the 1870s the telegraph was an important urban institution, and it cleared the way for the telephone. As the first practical application of electricity, telegraphy had broad appeal for intra-urban communications, especially since the greatest amount of commercial and financial enterprise took place in the central business districts and environs. In addition, private lines met rising demand for improved communications between residences as well as between businesses and firms. Investors were particularly attracted to the new urban telegraph services because of the potential impact on trade and because these services required relatively limited investment. Telegraphic communication accelerated the pace of business and created new enterprises such as national and regional commodity exchanges. It also connected branches of the same firm, so the factory could locate on cheaper land along the urban fringe, while the administrative office remained in the central business district.

Yet improvement in the flow of information often led to substantial backup of messages. The invention of the Gold Indicator (1866) by Samuel Laws, an engineer and vice-president of the New York Gold Exchange, and Edward A. Calahan's printing telegraph (which evolved into the stock ticker) helped to alleviate many logjams. By 1900 prices and sales on stock exchanges in New York City were being transmitted to more than one thousand tickers and businesses in the city.

The urban telegraph had many other significant uses. Widespread applications for emergency alarms markedly improved the efficiency of police and fire departments. New

York City and Berlin, Germany, for example, developed fire alarm systems in the late 1840s and early 1850s. William F. Channing, a physician and experimenter with electricity, devised a system that subdivided Boston into fire districts and he strung wires from a central station to alarm boxes located throughout the city. Before the Civil War several cities adopted the "Boston system," including Philadelphia, St. Louis, Charleston, New Orleans, and Baltimore. By 1892 more than fifty police signal systems had been installed in the major cities.

Application of the telegraph for domestic or residential use was for the most part less successful. Some specialized uses did aid the homeowner and apartment dweller. Edward Calahan's telegraphic call box (1872), installed in the home, enabled an individual to order food and other goods or call the police or fire department in an emergency. The invention of the telephone, a more intimate form of personal communication, eventually reduced the use of the call box.

Thomas Edison became a pioneer in the growing field of urban telegraphy, although he usually modified inventions rather than striking out in new directions. But as he would constantly be reminded, inventive skills without business acumen meant very little in the modern world. Finance, management, and marketing had to accompany technical improvements, new designs, and new products. His skill with mechanical devices and his innate curiosity were no guarantees of success. Edison's new life led him into a complex of business and personal relationships that subjected him to pressures far removed from the romantic notions of the lone inventor.

Although he had experimented with a wide variety of telegraphic inventions, his first successful device was the electrographic vote recorder, for which he signed the patent papers in October 1868. The apparatus had two switches or buttons that allowed a legislator to record a yea or nay vote instantaneously. Edison saw his market in the Massachusetts Legislature or possibly in the United States Congress. But no one would use it. As he was told in Washington, "Young man, if there is any invention on earth that we don't want down here, it is this."

Despite Edison's failure to anticipate his market, the experience proved valuable. He was able to attract some modest investment to the project. He also obtained a patent on his device in June 1869 through a well-known patent lawyer, Carroll D. Wright. And he learned that even practical devices are only as good as those willing to use them.

Undaunted, Edison was bent on making his mark on the telegraphic industry. Short on experience, he was long on self-confidence—a trait belied by his awkward, disheveled appearance and lingering hayseed style. At Williams's shop on Court Street, he built models of his "double transmitter" (selling for four hundred dollars). With his partner, George Anders, he also manufactured dial instruments to be used on private telegraph lines. He was performing in so many areas at once, however, that he often failed to make sound business decisions. Completing his latest invention became an obsession, and everything else took a back seat—even if it meant selecting poor associates, failing to manage his financial resources, or breaking contractual obligations.

Edison's most immediate success in the telegraphic field came in the form of an improved stock ticker, which printed the letters of the alphabet as well as figures. In January 1869 he assigned the patent rights to the device to two Boston businessmen in exchange for their financial backing. He then rented two rooms near the Boston exchange and with some new partners opened an agency that served thirty or forty subscribers by supplying current market quotations to brokerage houses. He set up a second venture, manufacturing and marketing his "magnetograph," which provided private-line contact between head offices of businesses and their factories and warehouses. He plowed his profits into other research.

Yet the work of the young fireball inventor remained largely speculative. He lived a hand-to-mouth existence with little guaranteed income and no major market breakthrough. But he continued to attract backing from local businessmen, as in the case of the multiple telegraph. He and his partners received permission to test the instrument on the Atlantic and Pacific Telegraph Company's New York-to-Rochester line, but it did not perform well. Since his business ventures in Boston were limping along, and because he had made some new contacts, Edison decided to stay in New York City.

New York City was the heart of the capital market and the center of commercial activity for the whole nation. The largest city in the United States with more than one million people, it was the leader in men's and women's clothing, printing and publishing, tobacco products, and telegraph invention and enterprise. Thoroughly cosmopolitan, New York City absorbed a constant flow of immigrants through its port, resulting in a society—as one contemporary noted—"composed of diversities of nations and customs, of thoughts and acts."

Upon his arrival in New York, Edison slept on a cot in the battery room of Samuel Laws's Gold Indicator Company. His benefactor was Franklin L. Pope, chief engineer of the company, one of two firms that dominated the service of providing gold and stock quotations to brokers in the financial district. The author of *Modern Practice of the Electric Telegraph,* Pope by the late 1880s became a founder and president of the American Institute of Electrical Engineers. While editor of *The Telegrapher,* Pope became interested in the young inventor who had published several articles in the magazine.

Edison's work with printing telegraphs provided the entree into the New York telegraph community. Samuel Laws was the pioneer in the field of financial reporting and the man who gave the young inventor his first job in the city. Laws founded the Gold and Stock Reporting Telegraph Company in 1867, which supplied price quotations for gold from the New York Stock Exchange to nearby banks and brokerage houses. Within a year, more than three hundred offices had come to depend on the up-to-the-minute quotations that the system provided.

Edison replaced Pope as superintendent and devoted his time to redesigning a printer introduced by Laws. The redesigned instrument was meant to compete with Edward A. Calahan's new printing telegraph used by Laws's rival, Gold and Stock Telegraph Company. Laws also had acquired an 1856 pat-

ent for a printing telegraph very much like Calahan's. To stave
off the competition, Gold and Stock bought out Laws's business
in 1869 and quickly negotiated an exclusive lease with the Gold
Exchange. Edison's patents were included in the deal—but not
his services. Calahan remained superintendent of the company,
and Edison was dropped.

In October 1869 Edison joined Pope and James Ashley, editor of *The Telegrapher,* in the new firm of Pope, Edison and Company. The partners intended to devote their energies to "the
application of electricity to the Arts and Sciences." Edison's role
was to custom design instruments for special urban telegraphic
services and to conduct research on new applications of electricity for fire alarms, burglar alarms, and other devices. The partners also established the Financial and Commercial Telegraph
Company, employing a compact printing telegraph that Edison
and Pope designed to compete with Gold and Stock.

It was only time before Gold and Stock took an interest in
Edison's business activities. In 1870 the company acquired partial rights to some of Edison and Pope's patents and purchased
the other assets from Financial and Commercial. By spring of
1870 Edison began to work with Gold and Stock. Marshall Lefferts, soon to be president, offered to advance him funds on a
regular basis for the cost of research and experimentation on
several projects. Edison signed two contracts—one for the development of a facsimile telegraph to compete with the Morse system, the other a printer like the Calahan ticker. These were his
first important contracts with a major telegraph firm. Gold and
Stock acquired the services of a talented young inventor and
kept many of his telegraphic improvements from their competitors. Edison acquired capital to finance a modicum of professional independence.

He completed the printer by April 1870 and continued to
work on the more difficult facsimile telegraph project. That year,
his new financial status allowed him along with machinist William Unger to organize a telegraph manufacturing shop and
laboratory—the Newark Telegraph Works. Edison also established the American Telegraph Works in 1870, which provided

him with a larger and better-equipped machine shop. However, Edison and Unger remained partners in the Newark Telegraph Works until July 1872, when Unger moved to New York City.

Newark had much to recommend it as a location for the young inventor's new ventures. A thriving industrial city of more than one hundred thousand, it had demonstrated early industrial strength in leather, carriages, silver plating, jewelry, hats, clothing, varnish, malleable iron, and shoes. By the late nineteenth century it added chemicals, hardware, cotton and silk thread, and enameled goods. There were an estimated thirty thousand workers employed in the local factories. The cost of doing business in Newark was less expensive than in New York City, and Edison was able to adequately furnish his shops. Supplies and materials were accessible and skilled labor plentiful.

Newark also offered an amenable living environment. Beyond the towering smokestacks was a small-town atmosphere. Perched atop a high flour mill, a writer for the *Northern Monthly* described Newark as "grand as every hive of industry is grand from such an outlook, beautiful as few cities are—and surrounded by reaches of hill and dale, of grove and broad-spreading plain."

During his five years in Newark, Edison operated several telegraph manufacturing shops where he worked on his contracts and manufactured an assortment of electrical products. The manufacturing shops became principal suppliers of instruments for Gold and Stock as it extended its business throughout the country. Edison particularly impressed his new patrons in 1871 with a unison-stop mechanism—one of his most significant inventions in printing telegraphy—which brought stock tickers in outside broker offices into alignment with the central-station transmitter. Although he had to devote time to the rigors of manufacturing, the contracts provided a steady income and resources for his experimental work.

In many ways, the Newark shops were precursors of the "invention factory" he later erected in Menlo Park, New Jersey. As his operation grew, so did his responsibilities, and he increasingly found himself engaged in the many tasks performed by all businessmen. In several cases, he left many of the daily operations in the hands of his partners. He boasted in a letter to his father, "I have one shop which employs 18 men and am fitting another which will employ 150 men. I am now what you Democrats call a 'Bloated Eastern Manufacturer.'"

At this time he also began to acquire a trusted and talented staff, many of whom later formed the core of his operation at Menlo Park. Charles Batchelor, a transient English engineer with a good knowledge of mechanics and considerable skill as a draftsman, excellent with detail and nimble-fingered, had the ability to transform abstractions into meticulous drawings. John Kreusi, a Swiss clockmaker and machinist, had previously worked in Europe and then was employed by Singer Sewing Machine Company in New York. He could construct almost anything, building detailed models from Batchelor's drawings. Two other key staff members in these years were Sigmund Bergmann, an excellent mechanic from Germany, and John Ott, a mechanic who served as unofficial assistant foreman.

At twenty-four, Edison was a demanding employer. He had the physical stamina and enthusiasm to work long hours, and he expected his men to share in the excitement, driving them day and night. At best, Edison's dedication was exhilarating to his research team, but his drive often came across as uncontrollable compulsion.

In the years at Newark, Edison became more systematic in his record keeping and sometimes in his research. In July 1871 he began to keep a laboratory notebook in which he recorded observations on his numerous investigations, new ideas, and random thoughts. Unger kept the books in their firm and Edison later hired business managers, although he liked to give the impression that the practice was more random. "I kept only payroll accounts, no others," he later recalled, "received the bills, and generally gave notes in payment." "The first intimation that a note was due was the protest, after which I had to hustle around and raise the money."

Several of the projects that Edison and his partners were engaged in required minor improvements to increase the efficiency of established telegraph systems. Renewed competition in the industry also led to interest in new systems, such as multiple and automatic telegraphs. Encouraged by several associates, Edison turned his talents to the automatic in summer 1870 with great enthusiasm.

Based on the original 1846 design of Scottish inventor Alexander Bain, the automatic telegraph was meant to utilize machinery and unskilled human labor in the transmission of messages. Using perforating machines, operators punched holes—representing dots and dashes—onto a strip of paper fed into a transmitter that sent electrical signals through the line. On the receiving end the signal was recorded on specially treated paper or by means of an ink recorder. Advocates believed that the automatic telegraph would be faster and more accurate than the Morse system.

In August 1870 Edison signed an agreement with Daniel H. Craig to invent an improved paper perforator for an automatic telegraph. Craig, former head of the Associate Press and an associate of Lefferts, was the principal supporter of the automatic telegraph. In 1869 he had obtained a financial interest in the system invented by the Englishman George Little and had contracted with the National Telegraph Company to develop it for press transmission. National balked at funding technical development, and Craig, who was dissatisfied with the performance of the perforator, turned to Edison. He was convinced that an improved machine would be of great value to telegraph offices. Edison worked on the paper perforator and other improvements while he was pursuing his various arrangements with Pope and Ashley, Lefferts, and William Unger. Somehow he hoped to keep up the juggling act indefinitely.

In need of more financial resources to improve the Little system, Craig convinced George Harrington, former assistant secretary of the treasury, to bring together a group of investors to develop and market the system. Harrington organized the Automatic Telegraph Company in November 1870. He also provided support for Edison to improve Little's system and to design his own in exchange for two-thirds interest in Edison's current and future automatic telegraph inventions. In October

1870 Edison established the American Telegraph Works with Harrington to produce instruments for automatic telegraphy, printing telegraphs for Gold and Stock, and other projects.

Edison had an opportunity to examine in detail Little's system and found it promising but "sluggish." He was confident that he could improve upon both the design and performance. In 1871 he devoted considerably more effort to designing his own system. By June, Automatic Telegraph Company was using his perforators, but they were not reliable and required further modification. His best instrument was the large perforator, which had individual keys for each letter, making it possible for an operator untrained in Morse code to work it.

Technical problems continued to plague the development of an automatic device. Automatic Telegraph did not begin transmitting public messages until December 1872. Although the system was workable, effective competition with Western Union required continued research and improvement. To that end, Edison received additional financial support.

Harrington retained a strong interest in Edison's work on the automatic, and he promoted the inventions in Great Britain. Edison agreed to go to England in April 1873 to demonstrate the system of Automatic Telegraph Company for the telegraph department of the British Post Office and to generally promote the idea of the automatic. Although the tests went well, the British did not adopt the system. They intended to improve the Bain apparatus and skirt Edison's patents. This was Edison's first trip overseas, and although it did not end in success for Automatic Telegraph, it broadened his professional horizons considerably. As he began to develop a sense of the potential markets for his inventions he was able to gain an international perspective early in his career.

Aside from his work on the automatic, some of Edison's best work in the early 1870s grew out of the multiple telegraph. The ability to send several messages along a single line—multiplexing—offered great economic potential to the telegraph industry. Different versions of the duplex, which could send two messages over a single wire, had been invented by research-

ers in various countries since the 1850s. Edison had experimented with the duplex early in his inventive career, but
without success.

Early in 1872 Edison actively pursued the development of
printing telegraphy. He formed a new manufacturing partnership with a mechanic named Joseph Murray, which lasted for
more than three years. In late 1872 and early 1873 he turned his
attention to the duplex. Western Union was an obvious customer, not only because of its size, but because Edison had been
drawn closer to the telegraphic giant. On May 25, 1871, Western
Union acquired control of Gold and Stock. The growth of Gold
and Stock's network had created a potential threat to Western
Union's own intercity system of commercial news distribution.
Under the new arrangement, Gold and Stock was given control
of Western Union's printing telegraph patents and its Commercial News Department. This made Gold and Stock the domi-
nant firm in market reporting and private line telegraphs, which
in turn made Western Union the leader in those fields. The
agreement gave Edison greater access to the executives of Western Union, including President William Orton. On May 26,
Edison became a "Contract Electrician and Mechanician" for
Gold and Stock, receiving company stock and an annual salary
of two thousand dollars in exchange for his patents on the printing telegraph.

Gold and Stock's purchase of the American Printing Telegraph Company was the final event that bound Edison closer to
Western Union. In May 1871 Frank Pope and James Ashley terminated their relationship with American Printing Telegraph,
marking an end to their business association with Edison.
Personal relations between Edison and his two partners had
deteriorated badly by that time. Edison had complained that
Pope and silent partner Ashley received the major portion of
their company's revenues. "I got tired of doing all the work," he
later stated, "with compensation narrowed down to the point of
extinguishment by the superior business abilities of my partners." Ashley did not share Edison's high opinion of his inven-

tive talents, later referring to him in *The Telegrapher* as the "professor of duplicity and quadruplicity." Pope, who some believed had suffered Edison's ingratitude, became a supporter of claimants against his former friend.

Edison's relationship with Western Union also grew as a result of the diverse approaches to multiplexing that he was developing. The telegraph giant was a modern business with a central management structure, which acquired and maintained its market position by, among other things, controlling new technologies. At one time or another, Western Union kept in its stable inventors such as Elisha Gray and George W. Phelps, and attempted to control as many patents as possible.

In the fall of 1872 Edison met with Orton and claimed that he could achieve the same success with the duplex at Western Union that he had with the printing telegraph at Gold and Stock. Orton was receptive to Edison's presentation. He believed that the company's competitive position could be improved by increasing the volume of business with the minimum of expense. This could be accomplished by improving the condition of the wires—increasing their capacity—and by stringing new lines to attract additional business. He believed that quality of service—not price—was the key to success. Therefore, Orton was as partial to the duplex as he was opposed to the automatic telegraph. The automatic system, he reasoned, was too expensive, delayed the dispatch of messages, and required skilled labor to insure accuracy. On the other hand, the multiple telegraph, which he had seen demonstrated by inventor Joseph Stearns, represented a potential cost savings, since more messages could be sent simultaneously and without less accuracy or speed.

In February 1873 Edison made a verbal agreement—according to Orton—"to invent as many processes as possible" for doing all or any part of the work covered by the Stearns's patents. By such an agreement, Orton acquired the services of a bright, young inventor on the rise and protected Western Union's investment in the Stearns duplex patent it controlled.

However, the promise of a multiplex system to revolutionize the telegraph industry became tangled in an intensified business rivalry and a full-fledged telegraph war.

In 1874 while working on the duplex in the electrician's office at Western Union with the assistance of Chief Engineer George B. Prescott, Edison developed a practical quadruplex telegraph. This device was capable of sending two messages simultaneously in both directions. A letter to Edison's patent attorney during the period contained a drawing labeled "Four-plex No. 14. Why not?"

The quadruplex was a major achievement. While Edison did not consider it as such, years later he still remembered the project as deliciously enigmatic. "This problem was the most difficult and complicated kind," he stated, "and I bent all my energies to its solution. It required a peculiar effort of the mind, such as the imagining of eight different things moving simultaneously on a mental plane, without anything to demonstrate their efficiency."

On its own merits, the quadruplex was a sufficiently portentous invention to excite the telegraph industry. However, two key factors helped to set off patent battles and inter-industry rivalries: First, while he was in their employ in 1873 and 1874, Western Union failed to obtain a formal agreement with Edison for control of inventions he developed with company funding. Second, Jay Gould, the notorious Gilded Age financier, became interested in the invention.

When Orton again hired Edison in December 1875, he had him sign a more formal contract. But Gould's involvement in the telegraph industry strengthened rather than diminished. He began his assault on Western Union by giving rights-of-way for telegraph lines along his extensive railway holdings to his own Atlantic and Pacific Telegraph Company. He continued his attack on Western Union by trying to use the automatic telegraph for a competitive edge. In December 1874 Atlantic and Pacific absorbed Harrington's Automatic Telegraph Company, which operated the Edison automatic system.

The last thing Gould used as a wedge against Western Union was Edison's informal arrangement with Orton over the use of the quadruplex. Edison had come to believe that Orton had little interest in the relevant patents, and he decided to at least hear an offer from Gould. In addition, he was in financial straits, having lost his house due to business difficulties brought on by the Panic of 1873. Orton sent a letter to Edison in January 1875, hoping to close the deal, but the inventor disclosed that he had sold his patent rights for the quadruplex to Gould.

Edison now believed himself free to work for Gould, having accepted the post of electrician for Atlantic and Pacific as part of the takeover of Automatic Telegraph Company on December 30, 1874. Much to his dismay, Edison found himself in the middle of a grim patent fight. In the court battles that followed, Western Union's attorneys portrayed Edison as a "rogue inventor" who "basely betrayed" his benefactors. Gould's lawyers countered by declaring that Western Union had tried to defraud Edison.

Gould lost the battle over the quadruplex and failed to capture Western Union's market. Western Union fought back by lowering rates, while Atlantic and Pacific struggled to expand quickly enough to compete on even terms. As for Edison, his standing as a businessman hardly benefitted from the scores of suits and countersuits that fueled the telegraph wars. By accepting Gould's offer, however, he was simply seeking a market for his invention at a time when he needed money and when Orton and Western Union were dragging their feet.

As an inventor, Edison's reputation continued to grow. In 1872 he received thirty-eight patents just for new models or new parts of his stock ticker. In 1873 he earned an additional twenty-five patents, several for original inventions. His quadruplex was a technical success. He also made significant contributions to printing telegraphy and acoustic telegraphy and developed new inventions such as the electric pen.

Thomas Edison faced extraordinary pressures as a result of his decision to become a professional inventor. His voracious reading and self-training, his persistent curiosity, and his determination to succeed brought him a long way from his years as a tramp telegrapher. He survived in the ruggedly competitive world of business in an era marked by wide-ranging creative activity. While his reputation as a maverick grew, so did his status as a talented inventor.

CHAPTER FOUR

Invention Factory

In 1876 scores of visitors gathered in Philadelphia to celebrate one hundred years of independence. The Centennial Exposition opened to great fanfare on May 10 and continued until November 10. This was the first grand-scale international exposition ever held in the United States, and it was distinctively American. The one hundred ninety-four buildings were erected in a beautiful natural setting that merged topographic variety, exterior space, and superb landscaping in Fairmont Park. Yet the aesthetics of the site was not matched by serious attention to the fine arts, to the nation's history, or to cerebral matters. Patriotism and material progress were the twin pillars of the event.

To many visitors, the present loomed larger than past glories or future hopes. Most people enjoyed the carnival atmosphere and flocked to Machinery Hall to get a glimpse of the latest mechanical devices and newest creature comforts. They were not disappointed. There were long lines to view Alexander Graham Bell's great wonder, the telephone. Elisha Otis exhibited his new elevator; George Westinghouse, his railroad air brake. The crowds also examined two crude electric arc lights, new gas stoves, and a fifty-ton locomotive. Less significant, but no less interesting, onlookers first saw linoleum and first tasted root beer, invented by druggist Charles Hires.

Without a doubt, the most dramatic of the mechanical curiosities was the muscular Corliss steam engine, standing thirty-nine feet tall and weighing six hundred eighty tons. Built and donated to the exposition by George H. Corliss of Providence, Rhode Island, it supplied fourteen hundred horsepower to run eight thousand machines in the building. President Ulysses S. Grant himself and Emperor Dom Pedro of Brazil led the official procession to Machinery Hall to start the great heart that would pump life into a host of exhibits. In the context of the Centennial Exposition, the Corliss engine was more than a machine. It proclaimed America's arrival as an industrial power, as a leader in innovation, and as a producer of tangible successes.

Thomas Edison was there, too, exhibiting his automatic telegraph. In fact, it received favorable review from the awards committee on telegraphy. Edison belonged among Bell, Westinghouse, Otis, and Corliss. Part of the "can do" spirit in Machinery Hall, he shared the optimism of his fellow Americans who swelled with pride over the inventive genius of the young nation.

Edison's presence in Machinery Hall marked his debut at an international exhibition. He was, however, already an inventor of note, and even more so at this time because of the publicity over the quadruplex. Soon after the exhibits were dismantled and the final visitors had left Philadelphia, Edison opened his remarkable research facility in Menlo Park, New Jersey, marking the beginning of his most creative (and productive) years and firmly establishing him as the nation's foremost inventor.

In December 1875 Edison had reached a settlement with Western Union on the quadruplex and signed a new contract to develop an acoustic telegraph. This capital allowed him to build a first-rate research laboratory. Menlo Park, a tiny spot along the Pennsylvania Railroad, twenty-five miles southwest of New York City, served Edison's needs in two ways. Isolated, short on distractions, and entirely under the supervision of the aspiring young inventor, it also was within quick striking distance of suppliers and major markets, particularly in New York City.

But Menlo Park was more than the site of Edison's most creative period as an inventor; it was a new home for his young family. Back in 1871 Thomas Edison experienced major changes in his personal life when his mother died and he married Mary

Stilwell. While his father, Sam Edison, remained vigorous and lived to a ripe old age—always with an eye to younger ladies—Nancy Edison slowly declined. In the winter of 1871, Tom heard that she was ill. He had not seen her in three years. On April 11, he received a telegram stating that Nancy had died two days before. All he could do was rush back to Michigan to pay his final respects. The loss was devastating for him, made all the worse by his long absence from home.

Tom Edison was then still a bachelor, living in a furnished room in Newark. What he knew of women he knew from the backroom talk of his fellow telegraphers and whatever he picked up in the streets of the big city. Rough-hewn and compulsive in his work, he could hardly be mistaken for a ladies man. Stories conflict on how he met Mary Stilwell, who came from a modest Newark family. Mary worked for one of Edison's ventures in the *Newark Advertiser* building where the boss's eyes continually drifted from the task at hand to the attractive sixteen-year-old. After a brief courtship they were married on Christmas Day, 1871, in a small family ceremony. Soon thereafter they took the mandatory honeymoon trip to Niagara Falls and then returned to a house on Wright Street.

The Edison legend—with an anecdote for all occasions—suggests that after the wedding ceremony, Tom left his bride and went directly to his lab, not to return until late into the night. While most unlikely, the story bears some truth about their relationship. Edison loved his wife, but work usually came first.

While Mary was intelligent, she was not prepared to become a wife, mother, and home manager. She had experienced few opportunities for the social exposure enjoyed by more affluent women. Very quickly, she had to learn how to care for a family, keep a house, and please a husband whose professional life so preoccupied him.

During their courtship, Tom Edison showed predictable signs of affection for Mary, and they adopted pet names for each other. He also exploited his hearing impairment for romantic ends. "Even in my courtship," he bragged, "my deafness was a help. In the first place it excused me for getting quite a little nearer than I would have dared to if I hadn't had to be quite close in order to hear what she said. If something had not overcome my natural bashfulness I might have been too faint of heart to win. And after things were going nicely, I found hearing unnecessary."

But things changed. Tom Edison was nearly nine years Mary's senior, becoming well known for his inventions and enjoying the notoriety. Early in their marriage, he made some effort to get her involved in his work but wrote in his notebook in 1872 that "Mrs Mary Edison My wife Dearly Beloved Cannot invent worth a Damn!!" Typical of men in the era, Edison believed that the public world of affairs belonged to men; the private sphere of the home belonged to women. Upon moving from Newark, he planted her in a modest six-room farmhouse in Menlo Park and expected her to pursue the tasks of a proper American wife.

By 1878 the Edisons had three children. Marion was their first, born in February 1873 and affectionately referred to as "Dot." Thomas, Jr.—or "Dash"—was born in January 1876 and William Leslie in October 1878. Tom normally spent Sundays at home, often using his free time to play with the children. As a prankster much of his earlier years, he tended to turn innocent games into mischievous, and sometimes cruel, ones.

Mary endured her husband's overbearing style, for she had little choice. She sometimes ventured into New York City with Tom, but the small Edison community remained isolated from the neighboring farms. Mary welcomed the arrival of Charles Batchelor's family to Menlo Park, which made the place seem less of a male enclave. Unable or unwilling to devote more time to domestic life, Tom agreed to let Mary's sister, Alice, move into the house. He also provided plenty of money as a kind of compensation for his long hours at work. While family life was far from idyllic for the Edisons, Tom allowed it to fit into his schedule as necessary for stability, comfort, and as a diversion from his business.

The laboratory governed his days—and many nights. Edison, who could function on a series of short catnaps rather than extended periods of sleep, often curled up on on a bench or table instead of going home for the evening. After particularly long work sessions, the staff would break for what beame a ritual midnight snack, when they would smoke cigars, tell bawdy jokes, or sing around an organ set up in the shop.

Since the staff remained relatively small, Edison enjoyed a close relationship with the men he called his "friends and co-workers." The "Old Man" drove them hard, demanded long hours, but had gained their respect and extreme loyalty. John Ott, who followed Edison from the Newark shop to Menlo Park, stated, "My children grew up without knowing their father. When I did get home at night, which was seldom, they were in bed." Asked why he did it, he added, "Because Edison made your work interesting. He made me feel I was making something with him. I wasn't just a workman."

While the composition of the staff changed periodically, dedicated men like Ott and the other Newark stalwarts John Kruesi and Charles Batchelor were essential to the Menlo Park operation. Some people noted that Batchelor was so deeply involved in the development of so many projects that when he was not in the laboratory Edison suspended work. Francis Upton, a newer member of the group, remarked that Edison, Batchelor, and Kruesi made an ideal combination, since "Mr. Edison with his wonderful flow of ideas . . . evidently always thinks in three dimensions. Mr. Kruesi . . . would distribute the work so as to get it done with marvelous quickness and great accuracy. Mr. Batchelor was always ready for any special fine experimenting or observation. . . ."

From time to time, new names joined the cast of characters. Within two years, personnel at Menlo Park numbered about thirty. John and Fred Ott were mechanics who both worked at the Newark site. Samuel D. Mott was a draftsman with artistic flair, who rendered detailed drawings of devices. Martin Force had little experience or formal training but became a valuable assistant under Edison's guidance. Francis Jehl, only eighteen when he joined the laboratory in 1879, became a trusted assistant. His *Menlo Park Reminiscences* provided some color about the work there.

In time, chemists and metal workers of various types joined the staff. Dr. Alfred Haid, a chemist, was in charge of the analytical work and the purification of chemicals and metals for laboratory studies. Edward Acheson, who later became world famous for the invention of Carborundum and synthetic graphite, joined the group in 1880. Francis Upton came in 1878 at the start of the electric light project. A physicist who studied at Bowdoin College, Princeton, and in Berlin under the famous Herman von Helmholtz, Upton supplied the sophistication in physical theory and scientific practice that was lacking. Despite Edison's jibes at pure scientists, he valued the help of Upton in complicated undertakings, and he greatly relished Upton's diligence and eagerness to please—which made his lofty academic credentials easier to tolerate.

That Menlo Park was becoming a business as well as a research facility was apparent by the addition of clerical and other support staff. Edison retained attorneys, who handled patent applications, licensing, and research contracts. Richard N. Dyer headed the patent department. Sigmund Bergmann of the old Edison Newark group formed his own company in New York City in 1876 but maintained close business ties with the Menlo Park operation.

Sam Edison helped select the site for the new facility. He also oversaw the construction of the principal building, a barnlike structure of two stories with clapboard sides. Over several years other buildings were added. The exteriors belied the power within. Edison had an enviable amount of fine instruments (worth in excess of forty thousand dollars), an extensive technical and scientific library, a chemical lab, an electrical testing facility, and machine shops. One small building was a photographic studio—later used for blowing glass bulbs, and another produced carbon buttons for the telephone.

Menlo Park quickly acquired monikers such as "invention factory" and even "Faustian laboratory," since it was the site where Edison and his staff developed the electric light system, the phonograph, and other marvels of the age. The imprint of Thomas Edison gave the place an incredible level of energy and intensity but also made it difficult to reproduce. Edison decided on the projects and objectives that the staff would undertake, and he had little tolerance for workers who got "sidetracked." With his finger in every experiment, Edison set the tone and pointed the direction for the research and development activities. Menlo Park had the scale of operations, the financial wherewithal, and the specialized staff to mark it as a precursor of the modern industrial research facility. As it operated in the late nineteenth century, however, Menlo Park lacked the work in basic scientific research of those later laboratories.

At the same time, the Menlo Park laboratory illustrated what direct corporate control of the inventive process could mean to companies that invested in research and development. Based on his previous experiences in Newark, Edison consolidated many functions under one roof. He merged invention, engineering, and production, with an eye to putting his products on the market and in use by targeted customers. He directed his work habits to suit the needs of a coordinated research team. And he gave attention to key business concerns such as fund raising, money management (to some degree), and promotion. Edison institutionalized the process of invention as no one had done before him.

Edison was a problem solver. He developed inventions by repeatedly trying his experiments in increasingly complex settings until he duplicated the item's actual performance. He worked in the mechanical, electrical, and chemical fields, sometimes employing a trial-and-error approach, but often working with variations on a theme. As Upton noted, there was "a marvelous accuracy of his guesses. He will see the general nature of a result long before it can be reached by mathematical calculation." And as Edison himself stated, "I do not regard myself as a pure scientist as many people insist that I am. . . . I am only a professional inventor. My studies and experiments have been conducted entirely with the object of inventing that which will have commercial utility."

Even when experiments failed, Edison concentrated on ends rather than means. "I never allow myself to become discouraged under any circumstances," he recalled. After conducting thousands of experiments on a certain project without solving the problem, one of his associates became disheartened. "I cheerily assured him that we *had* learned something. For we had learned for a certainty that the thing couldn't be done that way, and that we would have to try some other way."

Edison the pragmatist knew that making an invention work was only the beginning. Market acceptance was crucial. After his early experience with the vote recorder, he rarely lost sight of the work environment in which his inventions would have to function. In addition, as one expert argued, he was always on the lookout for novel and interesting ideas that he could adapt to his own needs. His problem-solving skills and his sensitivity to the market made him a successful, if not orthodox, business-man. And despite the public image of a folksy, rumpled country boy, by 1876 Edison was an experienced big-city inventor and manufacturer. It was no boast when he told physician George Beard that he proposed to turn out "a minor invention every ten days and a big thing every six months or so." Many of those inventions made their way into the marketplace, and at the very least, paid for more equipment, more overhead, and more free time to keep inventing.

Situated close to New York City, the "invention factory" had easy access to an important test market and an extensive commercial network. Edison, therefore, was well aware of the value of advertising. Although Menlo Park cloistered the staff in order to focus on the inventive projects, it drew curious on-lookers like a magnet. Edison welcomed journalists to the labo-ratory and always played to them for free publicity. They created the mystique of Menlo Park, uncritically reporting the wonders found within and magnifying the inventor's public image.

Soon after the Menlo Park facility was opened, Edison and his team moved beyond the work in telegraphy, which had dominated his life for more than a decade, to telephony. The development of the carbon transmitter in 1877 became a crucial element in turning the experimental telephone into a practical instrument for voice communication.

The invention of the telephone was the work of a handful of individuals—Charles Wheatstone in the 1820s, using wooden rods to transmit sound through the air; Johann Philipp Reis of Frankfurt, Germany, who used musical sound to create spurts of current that a receiver produced as notes in 1860; and Elisha Gray, chief electrician of Western Electric Company of Chicago, who invented a liquid transmitter in 1874, but who filed for a patent on the basic telephone mechanism only hours after Alexander Graham Bell filed his.

Their different approaches to invention—rather than luck or timing—distinguished Gray from Bell. A professional inventor and telegraph expert, Gray was apparently close to completing his invention on two occasions before filing for a patent. But only after Bell demonstrated the practicality of the telephone did Gray believe that a market existed for the invention. By then it was too late. Bell, by contrast, was not burdened with "the prejudice of the experts." Primarily known as a teacher of the hearing-impaired, he accepted an appointment at the Boston School for Deaf Mutes in 1871, and in 1873 became professor of Vocal Physiology and Elocution at the newly opened Boston University. His experiments with the harmonic telegraph led him almost by accident to basic telephone principles. On March 10, 1876, while testing a variable resistance device, Bell accidentally spilled battery acid on his clothes. He called out to his assistant, "Mr. Watson, come here. I want to see you." From the next room Watson heard the famous command and a practical telephone was at hand.

Yet public acceptance of the invention did not come immediately. At the Philadelphia Centennial Exposition, Bell amazed many people, but many more remained skeptical of the telephone's practical application. Exposition judges nonetheless awarded him a prize.

Bell had won only the first round in the commercialization of the telephone. A patent dispute with Gray and a market battle with Edison soon followed. Bell retained the patent but faced stiff competition in establishing a network. In 1876 Western Union rejected Bell's offer to sell his patent rights for an alleged one hundred thousand dollars. William Orton made this decision because the telephone as yet did not have much bearing on long-distance telegraphy. "What can we do with such an electrical toy?" he asked.

Once Bell and his backers began using the telephone to compete with intra-urban telegraphs, however, Western Union immediately snapped up Gray's patent. Orton also set Edison to work, hoping to get a jump on marketing a practical device and to prevent Edison from working for the opposition. Orton had long since learned his lesson about dealing with the mercurial inventor.

Western Union's financial support led directly to Edison's carbon button transmitter. Prior to moving to Menlo Park, Edison had developed an apparatus for analyzing various waves produced by different sounds, but he had turned to other interests before making much progress. By the time he returned to them, he was well behind Bell and Gray.

Once Edison attacked the telephone in earnest, he discovered the weakness in the Bell device—the problem of raising the volume. Ironically, the partially deaf Edison advanced the work of sound transmission that had eluded the teacher of the hearing-impaired. In Bell's transmitter, sound waves vibrated a permanent magnet, which induced a varying current in the coils of an electromagnet wound with fine copper wire. The signal was transmitted through the line and reproduced as sound waves in the receiver. The human voice, however, could only generate weak impulses in the transmitting device, and the resulting sounds were faint, made even fainter by the resistance in the wire.

Based on some experiments he had conducted in cable telegraphy, Edison began to develop a new transmitter and he also added an induction coil to the apparatus. In his transmitter, the pressure of sound waves on a carbon button (carbon had high resistance) varied a current flowing through it, thus regulating strong current sent over the line to the receiver, which converted the impulses into sound. A battery sent current through the primary circuit of the induction coil so strong electrical impulses could be dispatched along the main line to the receiver. Now sound could be heard over greater distances, the first step toward a long-distance system.

Edison's transmitter was successfully tested for the first time over a line stretching one hundred six miles between New York and Philadelphia. And although it took several years to get a patent, Western Union snapped up the invention quickly. Through Edison's labors, the telephone had reached its modern, usable form.

A heated "telephone war" followed. In 1878 Western Union enjoyed a tremendous immediate advantage through control of the Edison transmitter and the Gray receiver. Orton set up the American Speaking Telegraph Company with the dubious claim that it had the "only original telephone." Without an effective transmitter Bell was vulnerable, and thus he continued searching for an alternative to Edison's device.

The competition between the warring parties reached all the way to Europe. The war ended in Great Britain, leading to a settlement that solidified Bell's dominance. In November 1878 the Edison carbon transmitter was tested in England, but it was linked to a Bell receiver. Bell threatened action for infringement if Edison did not stop using the Bell instrument as a receiver. Rather than challenge Bell, Edison delayed negotiations to buy time to develop a new receiver. Bent on success, he pulled his men off the important electric light project and turned full attention to the telephone. Within three months, he found the answer—a chalk cylinder, revolved by hand or motor, which was pressed upon by a spring attached to a receiving diaphragm. The device was completed rapidly because it was based on the electromotograph, which Edison developed in 1874 as a substitute for an electromagnet in telegraph relays.

Edison's nephew, Charles, delivered the new invention to England, where it was demonstrated successfully before the Royal Society. However, the chalk receiver had not been refined sufficiently to make it dependable. The contest for English concessions now came down to which company had the shrewder business sense and the better sales pitch, since the equipment was roughly equivalent.

Bell had a good receiver but an inferior transmitter; Edison had a good transmitter but an erratic receiver. During fall 1879 Bell jumped ahead by using another carbon transmitter. And the British government sealed Edison's fate by moving against him in the courts in 1880. The decision in *The Attorney General v. The Edison Telephone Company of London* stated that the

Edison company's unwillingness to seek the appropriate licenses for operation denied it the right to establish a system. Curiously, the Bell Company's refusal to seek licenses went ignored.

By that time, however, the major battle in the United States was over. It was apparent in 1879 that the historic case in the Boston federal court, focusing on Bell's and Gray's conflicting claims over the invention of the receiver, would likely be decided in favor of Bell. Counsel advised Western Union to settle. An agreement negotiated in October 1879 acknowledged the validity of the Bell receiver patent. Western Union also agreed to turn over its telephone patents and properties to Bell in exchange for the exclusive right to transmit long-distance messages submitted through telephone exchanges. For its part, the Bell company agreed not to engage in long-distance telephone transmission during the life of the patents.

Western Union believed it had cut a good deal. In compromising in the competition over the telephone, it maintained its market dominance in long-distance message transmission—its primary goal. But, in the long run, Bell won unchallenged control of the American telephone industry. For his part, Edison saw his transmitter patent pass to Bell. However, he had previously worked out a deal with Western Union providing him with one hundred fifty dollars a week for experimental expenses plus royalties on any inventions relating to telegraphy. In the mid-1880s he signed an agreement with Bell telephone furnishing him six thousand dollars a year—a respectable sum—for his experimental work.

Edison may have shared the bewilderment of many Americans regarding the telephone in its early years. Few thought it had a practical use. The telegraph still impressed people with its utility as a business tool, as an aid to police and fire protection, and as a carrier of news. In addition, the telegraph left a permanent record. Therefore, telegraphy's hold over communications in the 1870s made inroads for the telephone difficult.

In time, improvements in the technology, wider distribution, and better advertising made the logic of telephonic communications clear. This most intimate of communications devices needed no expert operator and could send the most complex messages quickly and easily. The first telephones were installed as party lines between two places, such as home and work. By the fall of 1877 there were thirteen hundred such lines in the United States. The major breakthrough was the development of the telephone exchange, first tested in Boston in May 1877. Interconnection turned the telephone from a simple walkie-talkie device into a sophisticated form of communications. Businesses led the way in utilizing interconnected lines: internal systems in factories and office buildings, links between branches of the same company, and intracompany connections. In hotels, the telephone significantly reduced the jamming of elevators with scores of bell hops who shuttled messages from the rooms to the front desk and back. By 1909 the hundred largest hotels in New York City had twenty-one thousand telephones.

Ultimately, the telephone came into the home—first as a toy for the wealthy. In 1882 a residence phone cost one hundred fifty dollars a year in New York and one hundred dollars in Chicago, Philadelphia, and Boston. In the early 1890s the charges went up due to improved technology and the increase in subscribers. But by 1896 telephone service in New York dropped to twenty dollars a month. The average worker at the time, however, was earning less than forty dollars a month. As the number of subscribers continued to grow, economies of scale eventually brought costs down, and service charges dropped. Between 1896 and 1899 the number of subscribers doubled; in six years they quadrupled. By 1914 there were ten million phones in the United States.

Even more so than the telegraph, the initial technology of the telephone and its primary uses made it an urban phenomenon before it spread across the country. The original telephones of the 1870s could only operate over a range of about twenty miles. The first long-distance lines did not come into use until the 1880s and 1890s. By 1892 there were lines from New York to Chicago, and by 1915 New York to San Francisco. The industry, dominated by the Bell company and its offshoots, gained immense power and influence. Born in an era of great inventions, its broader impact on the American and world communities was just beginning.

As wondrous as the impact of the telephone would become, the sublime expression of Edison's originality was the invention of the phonograph. The idea grew out of Edison's experience with telegraph and telephone technology. His choice of the phonograph cylinder, in particular, originated in other uses of that form such as the chalk-drum telephone, cylindrical electromagnets and battery jars, and the electric pen. The cylinder was an important repetition of form that Edison borrowed from himself.

While working on the problem of telephone transmission, Edison explored the possibility of recording messages. His notebooks for 1877 show sketches of telephone recorders similar to his automatic telegraph system. In that year he designed an experimental repeater that recorded a transmission that could be played back for accurate copying. Like the Morse repeater, it used a recording stylus for making indentations on a paper tape. Several weeks later he turned to other designs employing cylinders or discs.

Edison was aware of the important studies on the nature of sound and hearing up to and including Bell's telephone, but he was unaware of Frenchman Charles Cros's 1877 study that set forth the basic theory of the phonograph. Cros, however, never built a working model.

In November 1877 Edison and his Menlo Park crew experimented with different-sized telephone diaphragms to determine their sound quality. It was common practice to mount a diaphragm on a frame with a mouthpiece, talk into it, and feel the vibration by placing a finger close to the center. Batchelor recalled that late one night after several such tests, Edison suddenly remarked, "Do you know Batch I believe if we put a point on the centre of that diaphragm and talked into it whilst we pulled some of that waxed paper under it so that it could indent it, it would give us back talking when we pulled the paper through the second time."

Kruesi prepared the diaphragm and attached it to an automatic telegraph wheel and stand. Batchelor prepared the strips of paper in various thicknesses. The instrument was placed on the table, a strip of paper was inserted, and the needle point brought down until it pressed lightly on the paper. As the paper was pulled through, Edison spoke into the mouthpiece "one of our favorite stereotyped sentences," Batchelor remembered, "used in experimenting on the telephone":

Mary had a little lamb,
Its fleece was white as snow,
And everywhere that Mary went,
The lamb was sure to go.

Batchelor then pulled through the tape a second time and they heard the nursery rhyme—"something that was not fine talking, but the shape of it was there . . ." The assembled crew let out yells and shook hands all around. They tried the curious device several more times, making various adjustments. By morning they had duplicated the sound almost perfectly, and before the next night had reproduced speech using a strip of tinfoil instead of paper.

Kruesi finely crafted an experimental device with a grooved metallic cylinder mounted on a shaft, which could be rotated by a handle. On either side of the cylinder was a diaphragm projecting a needle that could be placed into the groove on the cylinder and moved freely along the shaft. After more tests, Edison applied for a patent on the phonograph, which was granted on February 19, 1878.

Soon after the first test, Menlo Park was besieged with reporters and curious onlookers. The talking machine was a "nineteenth-century miracle" from the fertile mind of "the New Jersey Columbus," the journalists trumpeted. Edison was certainly the "Wizard of Menlo Park." The inventor loved the spotlight, thrilling visitors with all the tricks that the phonograph could perform. He even took his wonder to the nation's capital, making the rounds from the Smithsonian Institution to Congress and finally the White House.

At Menlo Park, Edison told a reporter for the *New York Graphic*, "I've made a good many machines, but this is my baby, and I expect it to grow up to be a big feller, and support me in my old age." After the initial publicity surge, however, critics began to mumble that the talking machine was little more than a scientific curiosity or a toy. Edison had little inkling of the phonograph's commercial potential, and by no stretch of the imagination was he ready to market it.

The Wizard's earliest hopes for the phonograph focused on education or business rather than entertainment. He saw the phonograph as a way to record books for blind people, to teach elocution, to record lectures, to preserve the voices of historically important people, to perform office dictation, to log telephone messages, and finally to record music. Having small children, he also envisioned the use of the phonograph for making talking dolls and toy phonographs.

All of these applications came to pass—and more. But the task of taking this invention from its primitive state to commercial success was more complex than Edison imagined.

During his early research (1877–1878), Edison investigated three different approaches—the rotating cylinder, paper tape, and the rotating disc. Enthusiastic about the initial success of the cylinder, Edison temporarily neglected alternative approaches to sound reproduction.

The only significant marketing activity in these early years was assigned to the Edison Speaking Phonograph Company. For ten thousand dollars and a handsome 20 percent royalty, Edison sold his rights to this company in January 1878. The firm manufactured the machines, primarily to be sold as music boxes, and licensed salesmen to hawk them nationwide.

Being enormously prolific had its price. Some inventions got a nudge from the Wizard, but were not fully developed or effectively marketed—as in the case of the electric pen. In 1877 he patented three versions—a perforating pen, a pneumatic stencil pen, and a stencil pen. Through perforating or stenciling a master, facsimilies of hand-written documents could be reproduced mechanically. Multiple copies of a document could be duplicated quickly and easily—up to three thousand from one stencil. The electric pen developed into the modern mimeograph. It was a good idea, but Edison decided not to manufacture or market it. Instead A.B. Dick of Chicago, a pioneer in the business machine field, acquired the rights and produced the electric pen and mimeograph for years.

During these productive years at Menlo Park, Edison was understandably preoccupied with monumental projects such as the telephone, phonograph, and electric light—enough for any one man in a lifetime—leaving few moments for serious evaluation on what appeared to be lesser inventions. But possessing great curiosity, he sometimes pursued interesting phenomena. One case in particular was the "etheric force." In November 1875, shortly before leaving Newark for Menlo Park, Edison saw a spark coming from the core of a vibrator magnet he was using in an experiment. He also noticed this occurrence in relays, stock printers, and the electric pen, but it was much stronger this time. Other experiments followed. This "etheric force," as he called it, was "simply wonderful, and a good proof that the cause of the spark is a true unknown force." He had observed radio waves, later to be used in the vacuum tube, the basis of the electronics industry. However, his own productivity —and the lack of a theoretical foundation for radio waves— limited Edison's ability to follow through on this chance discovery and intriguing problem.

The 1870s were innovative years for Edison as an inventor. Yet even when he devoted substantial attention to what he deemed the most important inventions, he had to give equal time to management, marketing, and the rigors of competition. Edison the inventor and entrepreneur was becoming Edison the major industrialist and big businessman. He had drawn upon the trends of the time to be successful, even if competitors sometimes had to nudge him toward the demands of the market. He had, however, made two crucial decisions. The first was to organize the inventive process in the same way that manufacturers and other industrialists were organizing their businesses, centralizing and specializing their operations. The laboratory at

Menlo Park reflects this decision. During his five years at Menlo Park, Edison obtained more than two hundred United States patents and developed more than twelve major patents.

The second major decision was to focus the research efforts of the laboratory on practical, marketable products with immediate impact on the urban markets of the Northeast. The telephone and the electric light offered sophisticated service delivery at competitive prices in areas of dense population. The business equipment was particularly well suited for large operations that could afford the capital expense and demanded high efficiency. Ironically, the phonograph, clearly the invention with the greatest mass appeal, fit into Edison's plan to market consumer-oriented products only after competitors showed the way. But while Edison the visionary faltered at times, the Menlo Park laboratory was well positioned to play a central role in the electrical revolution of the late nineteenth century.

CHAPTER FIVE

Success in a Cotton Thread

❖
❖

Cornelius Vanderbilt, one of the first modern captains of industry, died on January 4, 1877. The *New York Herald* reported that on Wall Street, "None spoke of him but in praise. Even those who at some time had suffered, owing to his manipulation of stocks, now that the veteran was no more, extolled his daring and admitted that Commodore Vanderbilt had not lived in vain. . . ."

During his eighty-two years, Vanderbilt had risen from a ferryboatman on Staten Island to transportation mogul, owning riverboats, then steamships, and finally railroads. Builder of the New York Central system, he acquired eighty million dollars worth of corporate properties by 1877. A rugged competitor, he went to any lengths to expand his enterprises—no matter what the cost. "Law? What do I care about the law," he once remarked. "Hain't I got the power?"

His public image was owed not only to his business exploits but also to his physical bearing, his passion for horses and sailing, and his philanthropies. A "consummate Philistine in matters of taste," one historian called him, Vanderbilt eschewed schooling and books, asserting the virtues of the self-made man.

To contemporaries, political leaders of America's Gilded Age paled in comparison with industrial magnates. Vanderbilt, Andrew Carnegie, John D. Rockefeller, and a budding Thomas

Edison were harnessing the great potential of the industrial revolution and pushing the young nation to preeminence in the world. They embodied faith in perpetual economic growth and material well-being so essential to the American Dream. There was certainly resentment of the "robber barons" and their exploitation of workers and the consuming public, but there was also boundless admiration. Few Americans were willing to wager their aspirations for a better material life on another economic system.

Thomas Edison benefited from that celebrity status in America's industrial age. His achievements at Menlo Park established him as a premier inventor and businessman. It was Edison's good fortune that his best known, and possibly most significant, venture—the development of the electric light system—was commercialized in such an era. He became interested in developing a workable system of indoor electric lighting in the late 1870s, which led not only to a practical incandescent bulb but also to an urban-based energy system with future applications well beyond the initial goal of lighting. In his own lifetime, Edison saw the city transformed by electricity.

Edison was thirty-one when he decided to devote his major energies to electric lighting. He had experimented with carbon paper filaments in 1876 and 1877, but he began a systematic assault on the electric light bulb and its complementary system in 1878. The moment was ripe. His background in telegraphy exposed him to many aspects of electromagnetic phenomena, to the mechanics of relays, and to the laws of circuitry, while work on the battery expanded his knowledge of electrochemistry. But he had little experience with arc lighting, the most highly developed technology at the time, and he had scant knowledge of dynamos (or electric generators), necessary to power large systems.

Still, his inexperience with lighting was more than offset by his general expertise with electricity. As an entrepreneur he could read the signs pointing to the practical application of electricity to lighting. Friends in science and engineering told him that a practical achievement in the field might be possible, which seemed to be confirmed by articles in current technical periodicals as well as increased patent activity. Before the abstraction could become reality, however, a durable filament had to be developed.

Key members of the American scientific community were impressed with Edison's ability, regarded him as a peer, and they would play an important role in his work on electric lighting. American physicists, especially George F. Barker of the University of Pennsylvania, encouraged him to take up the challenge. In the late spring of 1878, Edison was extremely tired and ill as a result of working simultaneously on a dozen or more inventions. At the invitation of Barker, he took his first real vacation in seven years as part of an expedition of astronomers to view an eclipse of the sun in Rawlins, Wyoming. Edison experimented with a heat-measuring device, the tasimeter, during the party's observation of the eclipse on July 23. Soon after, he and Barker traveled to the West Coast and then back to Wyoming for hunting and fishing. During the trip, the two men discussed the problem of electric lighting.

When they returned home, Barker convinced Edison to visit William Wallace, who ran the principal brass and copper foundry in Ansonia, Connecticut. Wallace had experimented with electricity for many years and with Moses Farmer, manufactured the Wallace-Farmer dynamo. In early September, Edison, Barker, and Professor Charles Chandler of Columbia University visited Wallace and viewed an arc-lighting system he had built. The small system included a powerful electric motor-generator—a "telemachon"—meant to harness electric power produced one quarter mile away. "I believe I can beat you making electric lights," Edison purportedly bragged to Wallace. "I don't think you are working in the right direction."

Edison nevertheless was impressed by what he saw in Ansonia and upon his return was bent on producing a practical incandescent light. He was entering the field of electric lighting at the crest of almost seventy years of experiments in Europe and the United States. However, the search for marketable lighting began with the use of animal fats and candles many years before then, and most recently with gas.

Many large cities in Europe and the United States needed some kind of illumination for public safety, and gas-lighting systems were among the first to fill the need. The early experimentation did not take place in the United States but in Great Britain, France, and Germany. The first American city to have gas lighting was Baltimore in 1816. During the next thirty years, gas lighting was installed in New York, Boston, New Orleans, Louisville, Philadelphia, and Washington, D.C.

After 1850 the gas industry in the United States entered a period of strong commercial viability, especially in large cities where central stations could provide street lighting profitably. Illuminating gas was the first centrally supplied light source that undercut candles and oil lamps. The illuminating-gas companies in the United States numbered more than five hundred by the time incandescent lamps appeared on the market. As in the case of telephone operations, traction, and other utilities, promoters of gas lighting struggled for city franchises, and prospects for large profits attracted individuals or groups interested in monopolistic control of the systems.

Arc lighting was the first successful form of electric illumination to compete with gas lighting. In 1808 Sir Humphrey Davy of England gave a public demonstration of his electric light, in which a bright, continuous arc bridged a gap between two pieces of charcoal connected to electric current. The commercial application of the arc light was not practical until the late 1870s, however, when several of the technical problems were remedied.

An Ohio inventor, Charles F. Brush, was instrumental in developing a technologically advanced and economically feasible arc-lighting system in the United States that could compete with outdoor gas lighting. He constructed his first public system in Cleveland in 1879. The new industry that Brush fostered became extremely competitive. His most serious rival was the American Electric Company (later called the Thomson-Houston Company), which dominated the market by 1890.

Arc lighting for city streets, a marvel in itself, demonstrated the possibility of extending electrical illumination into the home—a vast potential market. Arc lamps were too brilliant and too harsh, and their cost was prohibitive. Available illuminants, such as kerosene, had serious shortcomings. Open flames produced soot, dirt, and heat and posed a serious fire danger. The answer to these problems was an incandescent lamp.

In 1802 Humphrey Davy produced "incandescence," that is, current passing through a wire or filament to heat it and make it glow. Hundreds of experiments in the following fifty years failed to produce a long-lasting filament. Between 1809 and 1878, twenty types of incandescent lamps were invented. Frederick De Moleyns, an Englishman, was granted the first patent on an incandescent lamp in 1841. The lamp used both carbon and platinum. Moses Farmer became the first to apply electric light to residential use when he lit the parlor of his home in Salem, Massachusetts, in 1859. In 1872 a Russian scientist, Alexander Lodyguine, developed an incandescent lamp using graphite in a nitrogen atmosphere. He installed two hundred lamps in the Admiralty Dockyard in St. Petersburg, but they were short-lived, unreliable, and expensive. Many discouraged scientists and inventors abandoned the search as too impractical and too costly.

One inventor who refused to quit was Englishman Joseph W. Swan, who had been experimenting with electric lighting as early as 1848. In 1860 he made various experimental incandescent lamps using carbonized strips of paper and cardboard as filaments. But Swan abandoned his experiments for several years, discouraged because he could not achieve a proper vacuum in his lamps to sustain the glow of the filaments. In the mid-1870s, he resumed his work when the Sprengel mercury pump made possible a high vacuum in the lamps. On February 3, 1879, Swam demonstrated his new bulbs before an audience at the Literary and Philosophical Society of Newcastle. In the January 1, 1880, issue of *Nature*, Swam made his claim to the first practical carbon filament incandescent bulb.

Swan's achievement bedeviled Edison in the race to capture markets. In the meantime, however, Edison was consumed by his own furious attempt to develop a practical incandescent light in late 1878. On September 13, he drafted his first caveat (a preliminary outline of an intended patent application) on electric lighting, "Caveat for Electric Light Spirals." Based on his expertise in making and breaking electric circuits in telegraphy, he was convinced that developing a proper regulator could prevent the filament—at this time a piece of metal shaped into a spiral—from melting. In the caveat he described forty-four different regulator devices. He was confident that he was close to devising a practical lamp.

On September 16, 1878—three days after drafting his first caveat—the *New York Sun* carried a story entitled "Edison's Newest Marvel. Sending Cheap Light, Heat, and Power by Electricity." Edison was quoted as saying, "With the process I have just discovered, I can produce a thousand [lights]—aye, ten thousand—from one machine. Indeed, the number may be said to be infinite." He also envisioned a system whereby he would light all of Lower Manhattan, employing dynamos, underground wiring, and existing gas fixtures.

The story was repeated in other newspapers. New York financiers were particularly intrigued by the claims. The negotiations that soon followed between Edison and potential backers resulted in the incorporation on November 15 of Edison Electric Light Company, formed to support the experimental work at Menlo Park and to control any resulting patents. Of the twelve men who funded Edison's project, eight were associated with the telegraph industry. Some, like William Vanderbilt, also had been investors in gas companies.

Grosvenor Lowrey was central to the financial and business side of the enterprise. A New Englander who had fought against slavery in Kansas under the banner of John Brown, Lowrey established himself as an important member of the New York bar with powerful political and business connections. He became general counsel of Western Union and had cross-examined Edison aggressively in the multiplex case. Shrewd, but honest and congenial, Lowrey became one of Edison's best friends and one of his major assets in business.

Edison's new patents would be his major contribution to the company. In exchange for assigning these capital investments to the company for five years, Edison would receive stock, which would be worth a considerable amount if the inventions succeeded. (Edison Electric originally was to have three thousand shares, three hundred thousand dollars of capital stock, of which Edison was to receive twenty-five hundred shares.) W. H. Vanderbilt, his son-in-law Hamilton M. Twombly, Western Union President Norvin Green, Eggisto Fabbri (a partner of J. P. Morgan), and the rest of the original investing group contributed fifty thousand dollars each to the venture and became directors of the new company. They too stood to make millions if the project succeeded; if it failed, their liability was limited to their original investment. The financiers were banking on the reputation of Edison not simply to perfect the incandescent light but to launch a new industry.

Into October 1878 work on the regulator governed the activities in the Menlo Park laboratory. One type of regulator, for instance, turned attention to the behavior of the incandescing element in a glass bulb. Edison also devoted attention to the electromagnetic generator. In his previous electrical work with telegraphs and telephones, batteries were sufficient sources of power. But if an incandescent-lighting system was to function economically, it needed a reliable generator. In late December work on the lamp ceased as generator experiments were intensified. By the end of the year, the work in the laboratory became more systematic and Edison began to focus more manpower and resources on his electric-lighting project.

The Wizard began his quest not only to develop an electric lamp but also to develop related components necessary for a practical system of lighting. He drew heavily on his experience with telegraphy to visualize the system of relays and circuit breakers not unlike his multiplex. He first concentrated on the lamp, believing that the existing generators were sufficient to meet his energy requirements. He also focused on the search for a proper filament and other components of the lamp, which had baffled so many of his fellow inventors. Fortunately, Menlo Park relieved him of the problem of having to build new facilities or to assemble an entirely new research team.

Although the broad concepts of the research were his own, Edison relied on several staff people to carry out important functions. Charles Batchelor was Edison's chief assistant, and John Kruesi ran the machine shop. Francis Jehl investigated lamp filaments. (He later helped to set up Edison's New York operations and was sent to Europe in 1882 to assist in introducing the Edison system.) Grosvenor Lowrey advised Edison on financial and political matters and had the unenviable job of keeping the relationship between Edison and his financial backers cordial and unbroken.

Francis Upton, who became chief scientific assistant to Edison in 1878, was a central figure in the research. As a physicist and mathematician Upton was a perfect complement to the empirical Edison. Work on the electric light bulb, more than any of Edison's previous inventions, required precise mathematical calculations at key points, especially in circuit design. With the exeption of Batchelor, Upton became closer to Edison than anyone. And although the Old Man did not admit it, Upton's scientific skills filled a void in his own abilities and experiences.

In January 1879 Edison and his co-workers turned their attention to developing the light bulb itself. After considering other options, they determined that their incandescing platinum spiral could be protected from cracking and eventual disintegration if placed in a vacuum lamp. Creating such a lamp was made easier by the availability of improved vacuum pumps, such as Sprengel's mercury pump. But failing to obtain one, tests were conducted at Menlo Park to produce new vacuum techniques.

On March 1 Edison prepared a patent application for the vacuum techniques and high-resistance lamps. He had learned that lamps requiring high currents were impractical because of the need for thick (and expensive) copper wires to carry the current from the generating station to the customer. An alternative was high-resistance lamps that required no more energy to operate than low-resistance ones, thus allowing the use of thinner wires as conductors. Edison's later claims to the uniqueness of his electric-lighting patents was based most strongly on his use of high-resistance lamps.

Edison believed that he had solved the major problems of the platinum lamp in spring 1879, but more of the components in the lighting system remained to be refined or invented. Work on generators continued, as did research on other components such as meters, control devices, and insulators. This was a difficult time to concentrate on such a demanding project because Edison was simultaneously marketing his new telephone transmitter in England and working at home with his staff on the chalk-drum receiver. As a result, the intensity of work on the electric light ebbed momentarily.

Events in late October of 1879 changed all that. Carbon replaced platinum as the primary filament material, and a practical light bulb became a reality. Edison had experimented with carbon early in his research. He had tested carbonized paper as early as 1877, but it burned up almost immediately. He eventually turned to platinum because of its high melting point. One story suggests that Edison's renewed interest in carbon in 1879 came as a result of Joseph Swan's use of carbon cylinders in a low-resistance lamp. More likely, his own work on the carbon button telephone transmitter kept Edison interested in the substance. Also, the availability of the new vacuum pumps made it possible to burn carbon much less quickly than in the atmosphere.

The most significant experiment began on October 21 and concluded on the 22nd, when the team abandoned the spiral for a filament of carbonized thread. "The lamp was hermetically sealed and then taken off the vacuum pump and put on the electric current," Edison recalled more than forty years later. "It lighted up and in the first few breathless minutes we measured its resistance quickly . . . Then we sat down and looked at that lamp. We wanted to see how long it would burn. The problem was solved—if the filament would last . . . The longer it burned, the more fascinated we were. None of us could go to bed, and there was no sleep for any of us for forty hours. We sat and just watched it with anxiety growing into elation. The lamp lasted about forty-five hours, and I realized that the practical incandescent lamp had been born. . . ."

Documents from that time reveal no such dramatic moment. The Menlo Park staff initially viewed the success with carbonized thread as a promising new research direction, not the culmination of the search for a practical lamp. Early in November they tried carbonized cardboard and believed they had found a major improvement over the experimental bulb tested in October.

There was great enthusiasm in the laboratory as the result of the satisfying experiments. That enthusiasm, plus the predictable pressure from financiers anxious for results and the press eager for a story, led to assembling a demonstration system. Preceding a public display, the team lit up Upton's parlor, and two lamps were placed in Edison's house. Sarah Jordan's boarding-house, where many of the Menlo Park staff lived, was one of the first houses lit with the experimental lighting system.

On New Year's Eve people swarmed the tiny New Jersey community to view the new wonder. "Edison's laboratory," the *New York Herald* reported, "was tonight thrown open to the general public for the inspection of the electric light. Extra trains were run from east and west, and notwithstanding the stormy weather, hundreds of persons availed themselves of the privilege." Forty bulbs were lit simultaneously, and they were switched on and off. To a crowd accustomed to the flame of the gaslight or the coal lamp, this was an amazing feat. The turn of a new decade was an auspicious moment for the display of an invention soon to change the lives of millions of people. Edison had lived up to the headlines appearing a year before in the *Herald*, "Edison's Light the Great Inventor's Triumph . . . Success in a Cotton Thread."

Edison continued to seek even better filaments for his lamp. He captured the public's attention by sending his men all over the world in search of novel materials—bamboo from Japan, exotic plants from the Amazon and Sumatra. In all, he tested more than six thousand types of vegetation and had, as he stated, "ransacked the world for the most suitable filament material."

The drama of the public demonstration, however, camouflaged the real work to be done: Lamps had to be placed in a commercially viable setting. As a result of the demonstration at Menlo Park, Henry Villard, railroad magnate and soon-to-be investor in Edison's lighting company, wanted electric lamps installed on the SS *Columbia,* a steamship being built for his Oregon Railway and Navigation Company. In March and April 1880 the ship was fitted with more than one hundred lamps and four Edison dynamos. The lamps burned for four hundred fifteen hours—a successful field test. This was the first installation of Edison's system outside Menlo Park. It led to the development or refinement of additional equipment essential to commercial development including lamp sockets and safety wires (or fuses), and encouraged Edison to design a more elaborate system for a larger market.

Edison once boasted, "I not only invented the incandescent light, but I was compelled to work out all the complicated details of the machinery that is necessary to produce that light and distribute it in cities, towns and mercantile establishments." Indeed, in their amazement over Edison's success in inventing a practical electric light bulb, that part of the research was often overlooked by contemporary observers. Being a "system builder" was mandatory in the field of electric lighting. Little by little, as Edison was pulled deeper into the search for a practical incandescent light, such technical details as power generation, distribution, and efficient and sustained illumination required attention, as did economic considerations of cost and utility. His apparatus was to be the basis for an energy system of broad application.

Edison sought to invent a system because one was needed. Among other reasons, he found inadequacies when some stock components were linked to others that had undergone recent improvements. The imbalances and incompatibilities among the interacting components had to be corrected. The research process began with the design of components, followed by the structuring of a laboratory scale model, then a working model in Menlo Park (1879), and finally a commercial system on Pearl Street in Lower Manhattan (1882). Throughout the elaborate process to complete the system, Edison established several new companies to produce the necessary components in order to maintain manufacturing control.

Well-developed technology in gas distribution provided archetypes for many parts of the new system, especially the fixtures designed for lamps and the feeder-and-main mode of distribution. Gas was distributed from pressurized reservoirs through mains and into buildings through smaller conduits. Similarly, the feeder system supplied electrical power to the service mains through a number of smaller conductors—the feeders—each serving only a portion of the mains.

In the largest sense, Edison's conception of a system itself was based upon the gaslight. The nature of electricity also required major innovations in junction boxes, switches, and meters. The chemical meter, which Edison devised, measured the consumption of electricity at each household by shunting a small amount of current through an electrolytic cell. The meter was read by weighing the amount of copper on the electrodes.

Completely new techniques controlled the system. The fuse—or safety wire, as it was first called—and the fuse block reduced the danger of fire or overload from short circuits. New forms of wire insulation had to be utilized, including cotton coating and cotton impregnated with shellac, paraffin wax, or rosin. In 1881 Edison placed wires in cardboard tubes—predating metallic-shielded or plastic-insulated cables. Low-grade natural rubber for insulation was being introduced at the time. In addition, Edison devised resistance boxes and indicator panels to control and monitor the supply of power from the central station, as well as new testing and control equipment, a safety plug, and an array of lighting fixtures.

At the outset, Edison relied on generators manufactured by others, but ultimately he developed generators compatible with his own system. This was Edison's first major work with the production of electric current by mechanical means. Upton set to work on a new low-resistance generator. Although Edison publicly exaggerated the performance of his "Long-waisted Mary Ann" (or Long-legged Mary Ann)—the largest dynamo in existence at eleven hundred pounds—it actually doubled the output of previous generators, and it became the prime power source for the lighting system. The "jumbo" dynamo, a second-generation machine named for P. T. Barnum's world-famous elephant, had a capacity of twelve hundred lights. This was more than four times larger than the next largest incandescent lighting machine. The Long-waisted Mary Ann had a capacity of only fifty lamps. In modern terms, the output from one jumbo dynamo was 100kw. The Pearl Street Station, where Edison set up his first practical system, had six of them when it opened in 1882. Difficulties with the jumbo, however, led most of the early Edison power stations after Pearl Street to use smaller dynamos.

Location is also important in understanding Edison's electric system, since he and his associates envisioned a technology dependent on heavy usage, especially in high-density areas such as New York City. Edison's major objective to introduce central-station supply in Lower Manhattan certainly met with the approval of his New York backers and the press, who had followed his inventive exploits. Menlo Park was fine for a demonstration, but Edison required a setting where he could test a functioning large-scale system with all its problems and opportunities. A central station in Lower Manhattan, instead of generating plants or isolated stations used exclusively by their owners, could distribute electric light to the public. Steam boilers, steam engines, generators, and auxiliary equipment all would be housed in a single building. From the central station an elaborate distribution network would bring light and power to homes and businesses.

The first obstacle was more political than technical. Edison discovered that he needed the permission of the New York City Board of Aldermen before he could lay distribution cables beneath the streets. He also had to overcome the preference of some of the aldermen for maintaining the existing gas-lighting system, which they believed was more than adequate.

Lowrey made arrangements for the aldermen to come to Menlo Park on December 20, 1880. According to one account, staff members explained the technical principles behind the system and then displayed the experimental lights. Just at the moment when the aldermen's eyes began to glaze over from this low-key briefing, they were led into Edison's dimly lit laboratory. At that moment Edison clapped his hands and the room turned bright with incandescent bulbs. Set before them was a sumptuous feast prepared by the famous New York restaurant, Delmonico's. The aldermen were impressed. In April 1881 they granted a franchise to the Edison Electric Illuminating Company.

Edison's headquarters moved to New York City in February 1881. By May the small staff remaining in the Menlo Park laboratory shifted to operations in New York or went abroad. Edison's new offices were at 65 Fifth Avenue. At first his family lived in an apartment in the Clarendon Hotel, returning to New Jersey only in the summer months. But in 1882 he took a two-year lease on a mansion in Gramercy Park.

The Pearl Street Station was located in a three-story double building in the middle of a fifty-square-block area of Lower Manhattan bordered by the East River, Wall, Nassau, and Spruce Streets. "In my original plan I had 200 by 200 feet," Edison recalled. "I thought that by going down on a slum street near the waterfront I might get some pretty cheap property. So I picked out the worst dilapidated street there was . . ." Location was more important than the cost of the property, however. The initial distribution system encompassed a large part of the financial district, including the New York Stock Exchange, the great banking houses, and considerable commerce and manufacturing facilities. It bordered City Hall and Printing House Square, which boasted two influential newspapers, the *New York Herald* and the *New York Times*. When completed, the station accommodated six steam engines driving six Jumbo generators, each capable of supplying twelve hundred sixteen-candlepower lamps.

The most difficult task was laying the underground mains and feeder lines, which began in the spring of 1881 and continued until the summer of 1882. Although more costly than overhead wiring, Edison was most concerned with the reliability of his system. Gas lighting, which utilized underground distribution, had a good reputation for service delivery, and he was quite familiar with the drawbacks of overhead distribution—especially breakdowns due to storms and poorly insulated wires. The decision proved a wise one, especially when the famous blizzard of 1888 destroyed thousands of overhead wires throughout the city. Edison's men sank approximately fifteen miles of trenches for the wires, which ran along the existing gas pipes to the fixtures in the homes and businesses in the district.

"Wire runners"—telegraph and telephone linesmen— wired the home or business of every potential customer, leaving only the connection at the junction box to be made when the service was ordered. Following gas lines and wiring existing gas fixtures spared Edison's crew the problem of redundancy. The potential customer could choose between gas or electric illumi- nation without having to maintain two discreet systems on the premises. This was an excellent marketing tool for the fledgling electric light industry. However, the initial public aversion to electricity was not overcome quickly. The possibility of electric shock from the so-called "undertakers' wire" utterly frightened people.

The mains presented the greatest problem. Originally designed and tested at Menlo Park, they required considerable modification once in place in New York City. They were built in twenty-foot lengths of solid copper bars and bent into a half- moon shape. Two were placed face-to-face, separated by insula- tion, and set in an iron tube. The tubes were packed with hot asphalt, then laid in the trenches and connected by junction boxes. Because of the complicated calculations necessary to determine the size of the mains and the amount of power required to run the system, Edison could not start laying the mains until December 1881. City officials made the task more difficult by restricting work on the mains to between 8:00 P.M. and 4:00 A.M., so as not to interfere with daytime traffic and business activity. The practical problems of completing the sys- tem led to several missed deadlines and cost overruns. Edison spent $480,000, three times the original estimate.

On the first day of operations at the Pearl Street Station, September 4, 1882, 10$\frac{1}{2}$ miles of mains and 4$\frac{1}{2}$ miles of feeder lines were in place. By the end of 1882, the new central station served a one-square-mile area. At first, only one of the dynamos was operational, lighting about four hundred lamps; by October 1,284 lamps were in use. A little more than one year later, the system had 513 customers using 10,300 lamps.

Bringing the station up to full capacity required a breaking-in period marred by several problems. Generators had to be equipped with new engines, current leaks under the streets were tracked down and corrected, and wiring problems abounded. The Pearl Street Station survived nonetheless, and only a disastrous fire in January 1890 shut it down. Within a few days a reconstructed station was again in operation. Finally in April 1894, the station was retired and the building sold as new technologies began to force modifications on Edison's original design.

During the period of its operation, Edison had been able to demonstrate the viability of the central station concept for electrical power distribution. Pearl Street, in the heart of New York's financial district, could supply offices and workplaces, shops and restaurants. With such population density and a variety of consumers, it was relatively easy to broaden the market. Crucial to the success of the Pearl Street Station was that Edison never treated it as simply experimental; it was a consumer-based, urban-oriented, site-specific commercial enterprise. The electric lighting system and the station were parts of a business, not a technical curiosity.

While the establishment of new companies focused attention on translating inventions into marketable products, cost factors strongly affected technical and business decisions from the onset of the research. Beginning in 1878 Edison and his staff analyzed the costs of generating and distributing electricity. The benchmark was the cost of gas lighting. If their system could not be competitive with gas, it could not stand a chance in the marketplace.

All components of the system had to be evaluated in terms of cost, especially the lamp filaments and the copper wiring. The decision to find a high-resistance filament, in particular, was driven by cost rather than feasibility. A durable low-resistance filament could work, but the price of the copper needed to wire the lamps in such a system would be prohibitive. Massive conductors spread over a large area also would be expensive. A densely populated service area, therefore, was the best way to keep the cost of electric lighting lower than gas.

By applying his feeder-and-main principle to distribution, Edison reduced expenditures on copper. In the "tree" circuit, like the one he used at Menlo Park, the drop in voltage between the generator and the end of the circuit was reduced by thick, low-resistance conductors near the generators which became tapered toward the end of the system. The feeder-and-main system, with its smaller conductors, required much less copper. As it was, the amount of copper necessary to produce the Pearl Street system (180,000 pounds) was massive.

Once the system had been designed and preliminary operating tests had been performed, it became essential to employ manufacturing programs that could produce components in large quantities for commercial use. By turning from platinum to carbon, for example, Edison made it easier for his shops to produce lamps cheaply and in large numbers. Because of the many new components, Lowrey helped Edison to form several companies to keep manufacturing control in the inventor's hands. Edison Electric Illuminating Company of New York, incorporated in December 1880, was the operating company that built the Pearl Street Station. The Edison Machine Works (1881) built dynamos; Edison Electric Tube Company (1881) fabricated underground conductors; Edison Lamp Works (1880) manufactured incandescent lamps.

Throughout the project, Edison kept his eye on the market he sought to capture. Since the bulk of his inventions first went into urban markets, especially into big cities such as New York City, he recognized that many of the problems he would face in implementing his system were peculiar to the city. Besides cost factors, he had to contend with competition from gas-lighting and arc-lighting companies. He had to consider public safety and distinguish between the needs of business customers and residential customers. In addition, he became aware of a problem special to his urban market—the need to use electrical power not simply at peak hours but throughout the day. This would become an important consideration in commercializing electrical power. Shops and small factories required power to run their motors and lights during the day; residences would find the greatest use for electrical power early in the morning and at night.

To understand his particular market, Edison in 1880 commissioned a survey of gas-lighting use in the Wall Street district, including the amount of power consumed in operating hoists and other equipment. In addition, Upton and others developed careful calculations on power utilization. Herman Claudius took the work of the district canvassers and data from gas company records to develop block-by-block and even house-by-house figures for the energy needs of the district. The study also produced data on type of globes, problems with gas use (including leaks and impurities), insurance rates, and other energy uses.

The survey information proved valuable in designing the Pearl Street Station. Of course, figures had to be revised as manufacturing proficiency began to bring down the cost of lamps. At first lamps cost $1.40 each to manufacture, but were sold at $0.40 each in order to establish a market. For years the price remained constant, while the cost of manufacturing dropped—first to $0.70, then $0.50, and finally $0.22. While the consumer price remained constant, the average life of the bulb (originally at four hundred hours) increased, making them a good value. Changing lamp design to include sockets (first made of wood, then plaster of Paris, and eventually a metal screw cap) meant that the customers themselves rather than mechanics could change the bulb.

Metering schemes also had to be devised in order to determine a legitimate charge for the service. Edison abandoned an early plan to charge a lump sum for every lamp used. Only six months after Pearl Street Station opened did the company begin metering usage. The early meters were not always reliable, but technical improvements eventually led to better ways to determine the cost of service in the home, business, or factory.

Edison's development of the electric-lighting system, therefore, proved not only to be a breakthrough in illumination but the start of an energy transformation first experienced in major cities and then throughout the world. To Edison the research on the electric light had a more tangible outcome—a promising new business venture: "I had unbounded faith in the future of the business and fortunately my personal credit was good. So I pawned my future and, with a little assistance from two or three of my associates, organized and established the necessary shops to manufacture the essential devices that would enable us to go ahead with the business. . . . These shops entered actively into their respective functions in the early part of 1881, and thereupon the Edison electric light was launched upon the sea of business. The remainder of the story belongs to the annals of commerce."

CHAPTER SIX

Electrifying the World

The success of the Pearl Street Station marked the beginning of the electrical power era. It also saw the culmination of efforts to perfect the incandescent light bulb. The spread of electrical power systems surmounted many challenges. Financial reports show that for the first few years Pearl Street sold electricity at a loss, only to become profitable just before fire destroyed the plant in 1890. Investors in other cities waited to see how the new system performed over time. They were wary of the large capital outlay required. Thomas Edison traveled to Boston and Philadelphia, relying on his growing reputation and his powers of persuasion to attract would-be investors. But, for the short term at least, the uneasy gaslight companies remained entrenched in the major cities.

Soon after the announcement of the successful experiment with the carbon filament, however, gas stocks began to fall, and Edison Electric stock rose to an all-time high. One gaslight executive believed that "something ought to be done to Mr. Edison, and there was a growing conviction that it had better be done with a hemp rope."

The gaslight industry viewed Edison's handiwork as a threat to its very existence and waged a major propaganda effort to maintain its monopoly. It played upon the public's fear, noting that electric wiring was a fire hazard and claimed that gas light was healthier, increased ventilation, and sterilized the air. The gaslight industry also claimed that its product was cheaper than electricity and was more reliable because it could be stored. It marketed new fixtures in an attempt to highlight the aesthetics of flickering light. But these efforts were the swan song for gas lighting, as the incandescent lamp undercut the once-thriving trade. With the immediate future bleak, the gaslight industry was forced to seek alternative uses for its product, such as heating.

Companies developing isolated lighting plants posed another type of competition for Edison. By the spring of 1883, more than three hundred isolated plants were in operation, including one at the Blue Mountain Hotel in the Adirondacks (one of the first hotels to electrify) and several in Edison's own big-city market. Employing a lamp designed by Hiram Maxim—which Edison called a "clean steal"—United States Electric Light Company placed isolated plants in the Philadelphia, Chicago, and St. Louis post offices, the capitol building in Albany, New York, and on the Hudson River ferries.

Against his initial impulse, Edison began to develop isolated plants similar to the system on the SS *Columbia*. By the end of 1881 he established the Edison Company for Isolated Lighting, which ironically attracted the major portion of his business in the early years. Regardless of his commitment to central-station power, the businessman in Edison could not tolerate competitors stealing his thunder.

The commercialization of isolated-lighting plants provided new markets for Edison and stimulated innovations in the design of small systems. However, his major commitment remained to expansion of central stations. While raising funds was difficult, some expansion took place in Lower Manhattan with the construction of an annex to the Pearl Street system, located on nearby Liberty Street. In 1887 construction began on new stations at 26th and 39th Streets. The 26th Street station, completed in 1889, operated as a substation until October 1977.

Edison Electric stockholders were reluctant to invest further, especially with accusations that some Edison officials were getting rich at their expense. The banking interests under J. P. Morgan's tutelage urged caution. Morgan was intrigued by the new industry but was concerned that such heavy investment showed poor initial returns. Of all the financial patrons, railroad magnate Henry Villard had the greatest faith in the industry. But Villard had severely overextended himself and was in no position to help.

Some funds were raised through a new syndicate, but more promising were efforts to sell franchises and equipment outright through the parent company, EEIC. By June 1882 there were sixty-seven Edison plants lighting 10,424 lamps; the number more than doubled by year's end. Large Edison companies or utilities were established in Detroit, New Orleans, Chicago, Philadelphia, Brooklyn, and St. Paul in the 1880s. The inventor/businessman also played an active role in 1883 and 1884 setting up central stations in many manufacturing towns in New York, Massachusetts, Pennsylvania, Ohio, and elsewhere through T. A. Edison Construction Department. And by the middle of 1886, Edison isolated plants in the United States alone increased to 702 with 181,463 lamps.

The lighting revolution did not stop at the borders of the United States. Grosvenor Lowrey promoted Edison's system in Europe, with the financial backing and business contacts of the major banking house of Drexel, Morgan, and Company. Foreign markets were not new to the Edison team, and they assumed from the start that a successful lighting system would be exported. In Europe, central stations were installed in Milan and Berlin at about the same time as in major American cities.

One of the first important displays of the lighting system took place at the French Electrical Exposition in Paris in 1881. Charles Batchelor was dispatched to install and oversee the display at the fairgrounds on the Champs-Élysées. To power the system, Edison built a gigantic twenty-seven-ton dynamo (the world's largest) which was aptly named the "Jumbo." The exhibit began as a fiasco, with everything going wrong that could go wrong. In the end, the demonstration was a success, and it led to the establishment of a French company, followed by companies in England, Italy, Holland, and Belgium. The Edison group sponsored other exhibits at the Crystal Palace in London in 1882 and in Munich in 1883, not to mention lighting up Moscow with 3,500 lamps for the coronation of the new czar.

Edison sent Samuel Insull to London to supervise the work on the model station for the Crystal Palace exhibition. Edison trusted him to handle the details in England. Born in London in 1859, Insull had been a clerk for Colonel George E. Gouraud, one of Edison's major representatives in England, and worked for the Edison Telephone Company in London for two years. Impressed with Insull's business acumen, Gouraud and another Edison lieutenant, Edward H. Johnson, sent him to America, where the twenty-one-year-old became Edison's private secretary in 1881.

Sammy, as the boss called him, "tireless as the tides," quickly gained Edison's respect. In turn, Insull became a devoted follower. Insull rose quickly in the inner circle, founding and managing three companies and building the Edison Machine Works in Schenectady, New York. In 1892 he was named president of the Chicago Edison Company. In his own right, Insull became the leader in the utilities field, doing for the economics of electric supply what Edison did for its technology. He continued to expand his utilities through holding companies, and by the mid-1920s had one of the largest in the country. His fragile financial edifice was brought down in the wake of the Great Depression, an unfit end to a key figure in the early success of Edison's electric power ventures.

Edison had sent Insull and others to England to operate a model generating station as well as to set up an exhibit at the Crystal Palace. Interestingly, Edison's first central station was not at Pearl Street in New York but in London. The task was difficult, for the local gas companies had exclusive right to dig up the streets for general lighting, and they would not make an exception for a potential competitor. As an alternative, the Americans chose Holborn Viaduct, an arch that spanned Farringdon Road and some railroad tracks. Since it was a bridge, setting electrical mains in place required no digging. In addition, Holborn Viaduct had the advantage of being near the General Post Office, the Old Bailey, Fleet Street, and several churches.

In January 1882—almost nine months before Pearl Street was in operation—the post office, churches, offices, and homes near Holborn Viaduct were illuminated by electricity from an

Edison Jumbo generator. The installation, though not permanent, was a major technical success and was a testing ground for key elements of the Pearl Street system. While central station electrical power was slow to catch on in Great Britain, the demonstration eventually had a significant impact on systems throughout Europe, especially in Germany.

With Edison showing the way, other lighting and electrical goods manufacturers entered the field. In 1881 the Weston Electric Light Company, an arc-lighting company established in 1877 using the technical developments of Edward Weston, expanded its operations to include both arc lighting and incandescent lighting. It merged with the United States Electric Lighting Company one year later, bringing together the patents of Weston, Maxim, and Farmer. In 1883 George Westinghouse, best known for developing railroad equipment and generators, began to manufacture incandescent lamps. In 1884 the Thomson-Houston Electric Company entered the market and became a major competitor.

Technical improvements and changes in design followed rapidly. And the demand for capital reached a fever pitch. As in other new industries of the era, rapid growth resulted in patent conflicts, rugged competition, and ultimately, consolidations, reorganizations, and company mergers.

Edison faced a challenge if he was to remain at the head of the pack. As late as 1886 the manufacture and sale of Edison electric equipment was being carried out by five separate companies. Although they were interlocking concerns, they responded sluggishly to change. Eventually, the components in the Edison business family were consolidated to meet the challenge of increased competition in the field. In 1883 Edison Machine Works absorbed the Edison Shafting Company and the Edison Tube Company. In 1886 Edison Electric Light Company absorbed the Edison Company for Isolated Lighting. Edison United Manufacturing Company combined several of the manufacturing enterprises.

Consolidations and control were only part of the complex problems facing an infant industry. The heart of the business was the patents. These served as Edison's primary collateral for acquiring the confidence (and financial support) of the business community. Prior to the fall of 1883, Edison was reluctant to file suits for patent infringement in the United States for fear of giving away trade secrets on the witness stand. For his part, Lowrey believed that the patent applications were so poorly completed that they might not stand up in court or, at the least, were contradictory. By contrast, the major rivals routinely went to court in France and England.

The major patent battle in England focused on the Joseph Swan claim. The argument revolved around, among other things, the size of the filament—Edison's was thin, Swan's thicker. Swan argued that he originated the *idea* of a carbon filament, thus he had the right to the invention. Edison supporters claimed that their man had devised a practical lamp and therefore should prevail.

Both Swan and Edison had displayed their inventions at the Paris exhibition in 1881, and a public declaration of sorts— although hardly binding by law—shifted momentum to Edison. The American was awarded the Diploma of Honor, the Englishman received the Gold Medal. Edison's was by far the more prestigious award, and Swan concluded that "The jury had a difficult task to perform and I suppose they did the best they could with it." This was a victory for both Edison's prestige and his well-funded laboratory over the lone inventor.

Public approbation could hardly end a conflict that would net the victor millions of dollars in business. While Edison had 147 patents related to electric lighting by 1883, and Swan had yet to file his first patent until 1880, the English inventor put the opposing forces in a difficult predicament. Who invented what first was no longer the issue. Swan had formed the Swan United Electric Light Company, Ltd., in 1880, making a move that was certain to result in litigation. The British courts, however, refused Edison's application for an injunction, which made victory in a future trial less certain.

Given the potential profit loss in England and the bad precedent that an unfavorable court decision might have on business in the United States, prudence dictated a settlement. In 1883 the two inventors formed Edison and Swan United Lighting Company, Ltd., with sixty percent of the shares going to Swan and forty percent to Edison. They marketed their lamp under the name "Ediswan."

The new company solved one problem but raised others. Swan's work might negate Edison's patents, and competitors soon initiated legal actions of their own. In 1886, however, the British courts upheld Edison's basic carbon filament patent, which gave Edison and Swan United a near monopoly until 1894. For Swan this company victory was also a personal loss, for it diminished his initial claim to the invention and sustained Edison's preeminence.

In October 1883 a thunderbolt from the patent office set the battle in motion in the United States. The commissioner ruled William Sawyer had established precedence to an incandescent conductor for an electric lamp "formed of carbonized paper." The floodgates now were open, and between 1885 and 1900, the Edison group initiated more than two hundred lawsuits in order to protect the electric light system, less than half of which involved the lamp itself. In all, approximately fifty patents were involved, and the Edison companies spent nearly two million dollars defending their interests. Edison now devoted a great deal of his time to researching old documents, giving testimony, and being interviewed by lawyers.

The chief legal battle was the suit started in 1885 against the United States Electric Company for alleged infringement of the basic carbon-filament patent. The firm was Edison's largest competitor at the time. George Westinghouse had obtained control of United States Electric in 1886, pitting the new rivals against each other in the courts. However, after difficult and complex litigation, Edison prevailed in 1891. The judge held that the Wizard had been the first to make a satisfactory high-resistance illuminant out of carbon for an incandescent lamp and thus made possible commercial incandescent electric lighting. In October 1892 the Circuit Court of Appeals sustained the lower-court ruling. By the time the patent was upheld, however, it only had a few more years to run.

The emerging Edison empire remained under siege with patent litigation and internal financial problems, but it managed to survive. Competition, however, went beyond attempts to dominate a lucrative new urban market. At the core was an emerging controversy over the best and most effective means of generating and distributing electrical power, especially long-distance transmission. Edison had designed his central station system for urbanites, to serve a dense population with a wide array of residential, commercial, and industrial consumers. For the Manhattan site, Edison utilized local financial and human resources, relied on local workers and craftsmen, and evaluated cost factors in terms of local demand.

The central station was the centerpiece, but it also had great potential in electrical power distribution beyond the dense innercity which he had yet to explore. Edison's inventive sense encouraged him to refine the system he developed rather than to seek an alternative. He devoted considerable effort to rede-signing each component to achieve greater efficiency and better economy. He also exhibited stodginess in his efforts to maintain control of the business. Giving ground to competitors by expos-ing flaws in his own system or embracing a new one was court-ing danger.

But Edison could not escape competitive challenges. Lucra-tive financial opportunities awaited those who entered the new energy market. A debate over the merits of Edison's direct cur-rent (DC) system versus the merits of long-distance transmis-sion with alternating current (AC), championed by West-inghouse, centered on the best use of the central station concept and challenged Edison's dominance of the field.

The "battle of the currents" was a key confrontation in the fledgling industry that fundamentally transformed the world of power and light. In a country still largely decentralized, the DC system offered little hope of bridging the miles, and the iso-lated stations were only for specialized uses or the well-to-do. The low-voltage DC systems had distance limitations because they experienced "voltage drop," that is, the further the dis-tance a current travelled, the larger the voltage loss on the line. Long-distance transmission would require severely stepping up the voltage. But Edison, among others, believed that the transmission of high voltages was impractical and dangerous.

George Westinghouse, unwilling to accept the conventional wisdom, became Edison's foremost professional antagonist. Self-taught in electricity, he had worked in his father's machine shop in Schenectady, New York, for several years. In 1867 he invented a device for returning derailed railroad cars to the track, and in 1869 he invented an air brake for trains. The Westinghouse Air Brake Company gave him status as an important inventor and effective entrepreneur just as Edison's work with telegraphy had set him on his path to celebrity. In 1880, during a visit to Menlo Park, the two young inventors were quite affable. Only when Westinghouse turned to steam engines and dynamos the following year did Edison sniff a threat. "Tell Westinghouse," he said, "to stick to air brakes. He knows all about them. He don't know anything about engines."

Although Westinghouse did not have the expertise or the inventive skills of Edison, he learned to rely on those who did, seeking out bright young inventors and buying up potentially useful patents. By 1885 he was disenchanted with the commercial possibilities of the DC system. He believed that a system could be devised that could transmit electricity at voltages of 1000V or more, then reduce it at the point of use. He pursued the development of the new system despite opposition from several of his staff members.

The key was the transformer, which reduced high transmission voltage to safe levels by stepping down voltages at substations along the line or "bumping down" at the point of consumption. The transformer required alternating current, not direct current. The device, invented in 1883 by Frenchman Lucian Gaulard and John D. Gibbs of Great Britain, did not work well, but William Stanley developed a new one in 1886. In that year, Westinghouse Electric Company built the first commercial AC system in Buffalo, New York.

Westinghouse was able to transmit power at approximately 1000V as compared to Edison's DC system at 240V. The higher voltage not only meant transmission over greater distances, but costs could be reduced because much smaller wires could be used in the transmission circuits. Convinced of the limitations of the DC system and the promise of his own, Westinghouse believed he could compete effectively with Edison.

Westinghouse's goal was to produce a system that was more economical than Edison's, and with copper prices on the rise in 1887 he had such an opportunity. Since the DC system was well entrenched in densely populated urban areas, Westinghouse planned to capture markets where Edison was weak—in smaller cities and towns and in rural areas where customers were far apart. Westinghouse also had to contend with a direct competitor—the Thomson-Houston Electric Company.

Westinghouse and Edison each controlled a different portion of the market, divided along geographic lines. Edison was losing out in small and medium-sized towns, but Westinghouse could not crack the big cities. In total capacity, however, AC systems were catching up with existing DC systems. As of October 1888 Westinghouse had constructed 116 central stations (some DC stations) with a capacity for 196,850 lamps. Edison had 185 central stations with a capacity for 385,840 lamps. By 1891 Westinghouse surged ahead but only in the lighting field, since the AC systems were then not effectively designed to produce power for other purposes.

Although the future looked bright, Westinghouse and other companies that produced AC systems had to solve problems in order to compete on all fronts with Edison's DC system. The alternator, the AC equivalent of the dynamo-generator, was only seventy percent efficient. DC dynamos could achieve ninety percent efficiency. Alternators had to be designed to operate in parallel, like the DC generators, to save power input and to reduce wear on the machine parts. The DC system provided metered electric supply; an AC meter was not yet available. AC systems did not include a secondary motor, necessary to deliver power as well as lighting. This meant that AC systems could not serve industrial and commercial customers effectively. The DC motor not only provided power for industrial customers but was the mainstay of the traction business, further entrenching Edison in the major cities with electric streetcars.

The business rivalry between Westinghouse and Edison encompassed the predictable wooing of customers, squabbling over patents, and debates among experts. But it also became an ugly battle over the safety and reliability of the AC system, a battle that transcended the typical limits of market competition. Edison sought to undermine Westinghouse by discrediting the AC system through a publicity campaign in the press. Some observers viewed these attacks as the irrational action of an overwrought Edison stubbornly clinging to a moribund technology. But Edison may have consciously used these attacks to encourage legislation to limit voltages in electric circuits, thus undermining the proliferation of AC systems.

In 1887 Edison and his assistants staged grizzly experiments for reporters in the West Orange laboratory, electrocuting stray cats and dogs with high-tension currents. The Edison group issued a red-bound pamphlet in 1888 entitled "A Warning" that specified the dangers of AC, even listing by name individuals allegedly killed by high voltages. They also attacked Westinghouse and Thomson-Houston as "patent pirates," and pushed for a law to limit electric circuits to 800 volts.

At the height of the conflict, New York engineer Harold P. Brown got permission to conduct experiments on the dangers of AC at the West Orange laboratory. Brown intended to focus on the electrocution potential of electricity. As early as 1878 electric shock had been used as punishment at the Ohio State Penitentiary. In 1887 the New York State Legislature established a commission to consider humane alternatives to capital punishment, and it asked Edison's opinion on the prospect of using electricity instead of hanging. The inventor had spoken out against capital punishment at the time, but he did not dissuade Brown from conducting his own experiments.

After sizzling more than fifty dogs and cats, Brown believed he had proved the killing potential of AC and began to assail Westinghouse. Ironically, by the end of 1888 New York state was ready to adopt execution by electricity and turned to Brown—the man who was exposing the dangers of AC power—for confirmation that his experiments could work on humans. To make the point, Brown and his associates electrocuted a calf and a horse, and claimed they could also kill an elephant if necessary.

Based on these experiments, Brown sold an "electric chair" (using three Westinghouse AC dynamos) to the state for eight thousand dollars. In 1890 convicted murderer William Kemmler became the first man to be put to death by electrocution. Edison christened this method "to be Westinghoused." The battle of the currents had taken a grotesque turn.

The public safety issue clouded the technical limitations of the AC system. The Westinghouse group was completing work on a commercial quality meter and a practical AC motor, both necessary to make the system competitive with DC power. A workable ampere-hour meter, designed by Westinghouse's chief engineer O. B. Shallenberger, was into production by the end of 1888. Westinghouse now had the means to measure energy consumption of customers. A polyphase AC motor was not ready for the marketplace until 1892, but the principles for such a motor were patented by Nikola Tesla in 1888 and presented in a professional paper that same year.

By the 1890s electric motors were in use for several industrial purposes. Where steam engines were the preferred power source, however, the DC motor was not adaptable to perform those functions. To be fully competitive, electric motors had to exhibit greater versatility. Recognizing the potential advantages of a commercial AC motor, Westinghouse sought the patent rights to those currently under development. He began to rework the motor of Serbian-born electrical engineer Nikola Tesla for his AC system. Tesla, an "eccentric genius" with exquisite analytic abilities, had come to the United States in 1884 to work with Edison. Apparently Charles Batchelor had discovered Tesla in France, sending him to the Old Man with a letter of introduction. "I know two great men and you are one of them," he wrote to Edison, "the other is this young man." This recommendation, placing the young scientist in the same class with the veteran inventor, was just the type of remark that made Edison wary.

From the start of his relationship with Edison, Tesla did not want to be part of a team governed exclusively by the Wizard's technical visions. Tesla had discussed potential improvements in the dynamo with Edison, who purportedly remarked, "There's fifty thousand dollars in it for you if you can do it." Within a few months Tesla had worked out the promised improvements, and asked Edison for the money. "Tesla," Edison replied, "you don't understand our American humor." The young Serb understood well enough the limits of his employment and resigned. He soon established Tesla Electric Company to develop electrical inventions on his own terms.

Tesla is credited with the discovery of the rotating magnetic field in the mid-1880s. This led him to develop the polyphase induction motor, which used multiple AC currents to produce rotation. The practical motor built on this design was rugged, and it turned at a relatively constant speed regardless of the load. Although DC motors were easier to adjust and could run at varying speeds, the induction motor and its electrical system allowed long-distance application of electrical power.

Westinghouse had two great opportunities to display the AC motor and power system in the early 1890s. The best known was his lighting contract for the Chicago World's Fair in 1893, which he obtained by underbidding Edison. His system illuminated the "White City" at the Centennial with some 8,000 arc lights and 130,000 incandescent lights and ran machinery in a dramatic display of AC's potential.

More significantly, in the same year as the start of the World's Fair, Westinghouse was awarded the contract for the alternators and transformers to power the proposed hydroelectric plant at Niagara Falls. Until the advent of AC and efficient dynamos, the project had been impractical. The local community could not support the high cost of development or absorb all of the vast power to be generated. The new technology changed, and the expanded market made the development of the falls more feasible. In 1895 the first of three five thousand-horsepower AC generators was constructed. George Forbes, designer of the Niagara plant, described it as "one of the greatest engineering works in the world." The plant marked the beginning of large-scale hydroelectricity in the United States. By World War I, the new industry produced more than four million horsepower.

By the 1920s AC became the standard electrical power supply in the United States. The key to the broad application of AC power was the invention of the rotary convertor by Charles S. Bradley, a former Edison employee, who left the "invention factory" to develop the converter along with other related inventions. Patented in October 1888, the device combined an AC induction motor with a DC dynamo, thus making it possible to connect high-voltage transmission lines directly to the DC central station and traction distribution networks. Such an interconnection of systems offer great flexibility in the delivery of electric light and power.

The "battle of the currents" ended in 1889; the war had been won. Despite the force of events, Edison had a difficult time accepting the victory over his own DC system. DC power was not replaced but merely absorbed into a new configuration. Some operations still required the use of DC power, which remained a viable technology. But Edison's conception of the central station and its functions expanded beyond his ability to control the market. By the same token, the eventual merging of AC and DC also left Westinghouse to share the market, not dominate it.

Edison's business operations were forced to respond to the accelerating pace of change in the field. The final step toward consolidation was the merger of the separate companies into the Edison General Electric Company in 1889. This was not simply a change in form but a change in management as well. The control of the company shifted from Edison to a syndicate of financiers. Henry Villard and Werner Siemens, of Siemens and Halske Company of Germany, controlled more than half of the new company's capital. Villard was named president. Edison and his associates sold their manufacturing interests to this financial syndicate. Although Edison remained a director, he was weaned from firsthand participation.

Edison was a party to his exclusion from management, believing at the time that selling out would make him financially independent and allow him to pursue personal interests without the constraints of routine business responsibilities. He told Villard that it was important to push for consolidation as quickly as possible since lawsuits on the electric light patents were nearing verdicts. Decisions favorable to the company might give the stockholders an exaggerated view of the value of their property. An alternative view is that rapid improvements to AC power were undercutting the value of the DC holdings, and Edison wanted to move quickly while the assets were worth something.

In exchange for "money and time," Edison surrendered control of a large part of this new revolutionary industry and a great deal more potential wealth than he could imagine. If it was any consolation, by 1886 most of the pioneer companies in the electrical manufacturing industry were also out of the control of the inventors who originated them.

In 1892 the Edison General Electric Company merged with Thomson-Houston (second only to Westinghouse in AC power) to become General Electric Company. This action finally brought the Edison group into the AC field, albeit by the most indirect method. The removal of Edison's name from the company title was more than a symbolic gesture, since the merger took him completely out of the electrical power distribution business.

Edison had been a catalyst for change in bringing a practical system of electrical light and power to the world. Following quickly on the heels of the electric light was the development of electric heat and power for industry and electric traction for urban transportation. About the time hydropower developed, electrical power from steam turbines became practical. In 1884 Charles Parsons of England invented a steam turbine, and Westinghouse purchased the American rights in 1896. Soon after, one hundred thousand horsepower, steam-turbine electric generators were in operation. This new source of low-cost electricity competed with and then replaced nonelectric equipment. With the steam turbine and hydroelectric power, electricity had come of age as an industrial energy source.

The project at Niagara Falls demonstrated that central-power generation was feasible on a large scale, but effective electrical utilities did not mature until the turn of the century. The improvements in steam turbines led to the proliferation of electrical power generation, since thermal stations were more versatile than hydropower stations.

Manufacturing companies were major beneficiaries. A cotton mill was the first factory in the United States to be completely electrified in 1894. A dramatic shift from steam to electricity was under way. Between 1899 and 1909 the number of industrial motors multiplied by 580 percent and horsepower increased dramatically. By 1920 manufacturing had become the largest user of electricity in the American economy.

The adaption of electricity to manufacturing led to physical changes in the factories, which no longer required large water supplies for their steam boilers. Many industries could then migrate from the countryside to major cities. Decentralization of industry within metropolitan areas spurred the development of industrial parks. Electric motors also took up less space than did more cumbersome steam engines. Factories could be smaller and less costly to build, or they could use available space for other functions.

The cities also were the immediate beneficiaries of nonindustrial uses of electrical power. Electricity helped to encourage the development of tall buildings with elevators, lights, and sophisticated ventilation systems. Under the streets, water lines and sewers were run with electric pumps and monitored by electric sensors. Experiments with traction for city transportation were essential to the commercial development of the DC electric motor, and in turn, the electric streetcar was crucial to the rise of the industrial city and the evolution of mass transportation. By the turn of the century there were almost twenty-two thousand miles of streetcar track in the United States. The physical layout of modern American cities—dense central business districts surrounded by expanding suburbs—was due in part to the electric streetcar.

In the 1850s horsecars or horse-drawn streetcars had replaced earlier modes of transportation. But urban horses had a life span of about two years; they were ineffective in poor weather conditions, required constant care and attention, and were a major source of pollution. Cable cars, an alternative, had some success in the 1870s and 1880s, particularly in high-density inner cities. But the system never had universal appeal because it was prone to breakdown, posed extensive construction problems, and was very expensive.

The electric streetcar offered a better alternative. The application of the dynamo as a power source made a practical traction system workable. In 1879 German inventor Werner Siemens demonstrated the streetcar at the Berlin Industrial Exhibition.

In the United States the irrepressible Edison conducted some of the earliest experiments. He built an electric railway using his generating system during the day when there was a low demand for lighting. He set up a one-third-mile track near his laboratory, and he and Batchelor mounted a twelve-horsepower Long-waisted Mary Ann on a truck with solid iron wheels. They attached brushes to the wheels to pick up the current from the rails. During the formal trial on May 13, 1880, Edison's streetcar carried some twenty people at 20 mph along the bumpy trackbed. Despite the occasional derailings and more complicated technical problems, the president of Rockaway Railroad took interest in the project. There was talk of an Edison Electric Railway Company. Edison, distracted by other work, let the idea simmer for more than a year. He returned to the project in the summer of 1881 with the encouragement of Villard but failed to meet his deadlines.

Others pursued the development. As early as 1884 sections of the East Cleveland Railway were electrified. John C. Henry, a Kansas farmer and telegraph operator, overcame the dangers and inconvenience of electrified rail transmission with the development of the "troller," a wheeled carriage (later a rigid pole) attached to a wire connected to electrified lines running alongside the track.Charles Van Depoele built the first citywide "trolley" system in Montgomery, Alabama, in 1886. Black inventor Granville T. Woods contributed to the development of the "third rail," eventually widely used in electric railways.

The most successful pioneer in the traction field, Frank J. Sprague, established Sprague Electric Railway and Motor Company in 1884. His major contribution was a well-designed electric motor. He was audacious enough to accept a contract to install an elaborate streetcar system in Richmond, Virginia, which went into operation in 1888. Although Sprague lost money on the construction, he acquired valuable experience that led to several improvements in urban traction.

Sprague had worked for Edison in Europe, and he began to develop his streetcar while in the famous inventor's employ. Although the Electric Railway Company of America (incorporated in 1883) carried on development work based on the patents of Edison and Stephen Field, Edison took little interest in the venture. And while Sprague would have worked on the project under Edison's guidance, the Wizard would not give him freedom of inquiry. Edison's relationship with Sprague was a story often repeated in the laboratory with other talented subordinates turned rivals. Sprague decided to go it alone.

Few could have foreseen the dramatic impact of the race to find an incandescent lamp on life in the city and eventually on farms. Electrical power created heat and light and ran the largest motors and the smallest appliances. By 1890 it was possible to order an electric iron, an electric coffee pot, or an electric sewing machine, and by 1920 an electric stove, washing machine, dishwasher, vaccum cleaner, and hair dryer. As a new force in the business world, the electric power industry grew by giant steps. In 1890 the annual sales of the three largest electrical manufacturers topped twenty-five million dollars, with well over one thousand central stations in operation across the country. Between 1902 and 1929 output of electrical power increased more than nineteenfold. And by 1927 about two-third of all American families had electrical power.

Thomas Edison was at the heart of the passage into the electrical age—often as an innovator, sometimes as an antagonist, but never merely as an observer. Years of heady activity in the 1880s and early 1890s marked a peak in his inventive career. But it was difficult to imagine that what followed could be anticlimactic for a man who had barely entered his fortieth year.

CHAPTER SEVEN

Gilded Age Industrialist

"In the name of the people of Illinois, I command this meeting immediately and peaceably to disperse," demanded Chicago Police Captain William Ward, standing at the head of 180 troops. Radical labor leaders stepped down from the wagon in Haymarket Square where they had been leading a rally of about twelve hundred people in support of brother strikers. Suddenly a flickering dynamite bomb flew out of the crowd, landing at the feet of the police phalanx. Several officers went down, but those still standing quickly returned fire in all directions. When the chaos finally ended, eight policemen and four workers lay dead with scores of others wounded and everyone else badly shaken.

The Haymarket riot took place on May 4, 1886, on the heels of demands for an eight-hour day from the national trade unions. It came at the end of a decade of labor unrest which extended from the coal fields to the railroads and into the heart of every major city. Employers fiercely resisted the organization of its workers, receiving strong support from government and the public for protecting the fruits of the laissez faire economy.

News of the bombing aroused anti-union hysteria and inspired a call for action against labor radicalism. The Haymarket riot linked anarchism with labor in the public mind, fed the fears of mass immigration, and—temporarily at least—weakened the national labor movement. Faith in the American Dream, the efforts of labor unions, the general affluence of the nation, and some timely legislation changed the lot of the worker in the twentieth century. But during the lifetime of Thomas Edison it was a businessman's world, not a worker's paradise. While Edison had known what it was like to work for someone else, he was among the fortunate few who crossed the line from employed to employer. In striving to become a professional inventor he also became a businessman, succeeding in marketing his products in the same cities where the labor unions struggled for survival.

The year of the Haymarket riot, 1886, was particularly auspicious for Edison the industrialist. Seemingly impervious to the social upheavals of the day, he was basking in the acclaim of his newest inventions and was nearing completion of his magnificent new complex in West Orange, New Jersey, which would become the greatest industrial research facility in the nation.

Edison had not simply outgrown the space of the Menlo Park laboratory, but also its capabilities. His career now pointed toward manufacturing, and his desire to own factories complemented the need for a good laboratory. As countless enterprises piled up over the years, the hours required to manage the businesses, market the products, and fight the chronic legal battles commanded more of the inventor's time. Since Menlo Park he had passed into a new phase of professional life—less the bright, inventive genius under the wing of Jay Gould and J. P. Morgan, and more the maturing capitalist under the pressure of deadlines and details.

Edison's personal life also changed dramatically in the mid-1880s. Mary died on August 9, 1884, leaving him a widower at thirty-seven. While no one questioned his strong attachment to her, few regarded him as an ideal husband. As he rose in stature as an inventor, he provided liberally for Mary with material goods but was not so generous with his time. Distracted by work, he often pored over technical journals while at home or turned brief attention to the children on a Sunday afternoon.

He never regarded Mary as an equal. To Edison, women were by their very nature mentally inferior, and his wife's role was to support him in any way she could. Mary fit the box which her husband constructed, staying clear of his business ventures, tending—if not overindulging—the children, and looking after the affairs of the house.

Mary was a lonely woman, grew plump on chocolates, and was frequently ill. Trips to Brooklyn (where her family now lived) or summers at the shore were only slight diversions. Even the move to New York in 1881, which took her out of the countryside, did not change her daily routine. When Mary Stillwell Edison died at the age of twenty-nine, Tom told people that it was typhoid. But some have suspected that it was a brain tumor, aggravated by the unsettling stress in her life.

As a young widower and a millionaire, Edison was not likely to remain a bachelor for long. By the customs of the day, it was perfectly acceptable for him to consider remarriage as soon as possible. His secretary, Samuel Insull, was kept busy answering the correspondence of sympathetic, and eligible, women. His friends, the Ezra T. Gillilands, acted as matchmakers. (Ezra was a minor inventor of telegraphic equipment who had built a successful business in Boston. He and Edison had significant business connections going back to their days in telegraphy.) They invited scores of potential mates to meet the famous inventor at their home. Edison wrote to Insull, "Come to Boston. At Gill's house there are lots of pretty girls."

The woman who caught his eye was a stunning brunette, Mina Miller. The Millers were friends of the Gillilands from Akron, Ohio, where Lewis Miller was a wealthy farm tool manufacturer, a philanthropist, and cofounder of the Chautauqua Association. Mina had gone to finishing school in Boston and had toured Europe. Like her father, she was involved in charity work and was deeply religious. Where Mary was gentle, Mina tended to be stronger willed, more inclined to assert her views while observing the public decorum required in the late nineteenth century.

Tom and Mina first met in the winter of 1885 at the Gilliland home. She was nineteen at the time, and he was immediately smitten. A budding courtship was delayed, however, when Edison caught a cold—which turned into pneumonia—while on business in Chicago. He was gravely ill, more so than he allowed himself to admit, but finally agreed to recuperate in Florida. He left Chicago for St. Augustine with his daughter Marion, and the Gillilands immediately followed.

The stay in Florida was extended because Edison saw an opportunity to track down bamboo and other exotic plant fibers suitable as filaments for his incandescent lamp in the Everglades and the Keys. Revived by his convalescence and exhilarated over the wealth of plant life, he took an option on a thirteen-acre plot along the Caloosahatchee River near Fort Myers. This became the site for his winter home which he frequented regularly.

Upon returning to New York, his thoughts were filled with Mina, so much so that Marion became fiercely jealous of the rival for her father's affections. But once Edison had made up his mind, he was bent on marrying "the Maid of Chautauqua" as he called her, despite his daughter's feelings.

The Miller family was reticent to say the least. Their upright daughter, raised in the proper religious environment, was being courted by a much older, brash man of questionable religious conviction. But Edison's public stature and the wishes of their daughter won out. Tom and Mina were married by a leading Methodist minister under an arch of roses in the Miller home on February 24, 1886.

Befitting his new bride and his new station in life, Edison bought a sprawling mansion in the famous planned development of Llewellyn Park in West Orange, New Jersey. The scenic Orange Valley was a resort area for citizens of Newark and only twelve miles west of New York City. Built by a New York merchant at the immense cost of about two hundred thousand dollars, "Glenmont" was a garish brick and wood giant of the Queen Anne style with cavernous rooms, several outbuildings, and expansive gardens. It sat on a knoll surrounded by eleven wooded acres. Hardly the setting in which one would expect to find the rough-hewn Edison, it suited Mina well and it clearly reflected the nouveau riche tastes of the day. As biographer

Matthew Josephson noted, the house signalized "the status and power of the princes of oil, pork, iron, coal, railroads, and (now) electricity."

The newlyweds moved into Glenmont after returning from Florida. With a new wife, two new homes, and a soon-to-be completed research and manufacturing facility, Edison was embarking on life at middle age. Unlike Mary, Mina was not content to let her husband carry on as he wished. She wanted to polish this rough jewel. "You have no idea," she later remarked, "what it means to be married to a great man." Despite the likely tension that such determination could create, Mina was a loyal supporter of Tom's ventures, and he was an affectionate husband. Inevitably, work came first over family, but their relationship remained steady and strong.

The place of the children in this new marriage was sometimes ill-defined and uneasy. Mary's children never really enjoyed staying at Glenmont. Marion was too close in age to Mina and too attached to her father for much to come of the relationship. She attended boarding school or traveled in Europe. The boys spent a great deal of time with their aunt in Menlo Park or on Uncle Pitt's farm in Michigan. Tom and Mina had three children of their own—Madeleine born in 1888; Charles in 1890; and Theodore in 1898. Neither parent devoted much attention to them, however. In later life Mina regretted that choice more than her husband did, and she changed her ways.

Mina had staff to care for the children, and she kept busy in the community. She was very active with the Red Cross, the Missionary Services, Daughters of the American Revolution, the arts, and her church. A less resilient and resourceful woman might have been unhappy, but Mina filled her time with activities to compensate for the long absences of her husband.

Even as his stature and celebrity grew, Edison never lost his taste for hard work. His goal in building the West Orange facility was to fashion a grander Menlo Park with an emphasis on manufacturing. As he told friends, he wanted to fabricate "anything from a lady's watch to a locomotive." "Inventions that formerly took months & cost large sums," he wrote in his notebook, "can now be done 2 or 3 days with very small expense, as I shall carry a stock of almost every conceivable material."

These goals suggest a remarkable consistency with his plans for Menlo Park ten years earlier: "a minor invention every ten days and a big thing every six months or so." The clearest difference was the greater emphasis on manufacturing, especially consumer goods for the urban market. He wanted to make "useful things that every man, woman and child in the world wants." Such products required less capital and held out the promise of higher profits than the complex lighting and power systems that had monopolized his time and drained his energies. The fourteen-acre site of the new laboratory and manufacturing complex, meant to be the largest and best in the world, was one-half mile from Glenmont on Main Street in the small village of West Orange. Without venturing far up the street, an onlooker could view Manhattan Island across the short expanse of harbor separating New Jersey from New York.

Edison was constantly milling around the construction site—volunteering advice, harassing lazy workers, and changing plans. Understandably, he was trying to protect his healthy investment in the facilities, which cost $180,000 to build. The project was developed with inventive versatility and manufacturing scale in mind. The laboratory had to allow Edison to work on several projects at once; the manufacturing facilities had to be sufficiently expansive to meet the needs of a mass market. Charles Batchelor prepared the initial drawings for the laboratory—which would be the largest private laboratory in the world. Architect Henry Holly, who had designed Glenmont, completed the formal plans.

The building was three-story red brick with an attached powerhouse of more than fifty thousand square feet of floor space. The first two floors were primarily occupied by machine shops, with a third floor devoted to phonographic and photographic departments. The building also housed an engine room, stock rooms, glass-blowing and pumping facilities, and space for electrical testing. The west end was a two-and-one-half-story library. This was where the Wizard spent much of his time—sitting at a huge desk, conducting the business of his growing empire.

Edison often tinkered with the layout of the workspace to maximize its utility and to accommodate changes to meet the demands of new projects. Even with the constant transformation of space, the impressive laboratory was not sufficient for his plans. Edison soon authorized the construction of four additional work areas—Building 1, devoted to electrical work and magnetism; Building 2, a chemical laboratory; Building 3, a woodworking shop; and Building 4, a metallurgical laboratory. These long, one-story structures were at right angles to the main building, forming a quadrangle at the center.

The plan for the site was completed with a clear understanding that the laboratory could not be separated from the industrial components. Research and fabrication went hand in hand. The whole facility was fenced and patrolled by a guard. The openness of Menlo Park was replaced by controlled access, with experiments often cloaked in secrecy to protect company interests. This did not keep Edison from inviting numerous reporters and potential investors to tour the facilities as a way of promoting new inventions and products, and acquiring essential operating funds.

The insides were as important as the outsides, and Edison stocked his new facility with an exhaustive list of chemicals, minerals, tools, scientific apparati, ten thousand volumes for his library, and every other type of material available—"everything from an elephant's hide to the eyeballs of a United States senator." There was so much equipment that the original machine shop was divided in two—one for heavy tools and another for precision tools. Experimental equipment of all types was moved into the various laboratories. Supplies were amassed in storerooms to insure that the widest range of experimentation could take place without loss of precious time waiting for orders to arrive.

The staff, with a core of twenty or thirty men, ballooned well above that number, depending on the projects. It was a diverse group like his Menlo Park gang, but it also included a horde of operatives to replicate production items in batches. Batchelor, the Otts, and others of long standing were there. Edison added chemical consultant J. W. Aylsworth, chemist (and later inventor) Reginald Fessenden, and Arthur E. Kennelly, a gifted mathematician, who became chief electrician at West Orange and later had a successful career as an electrical engineer and academic. The work force also included university-trained engineers, draftsmen, mechanical assistants, clerks and bookkeepers, and good general experimenters whom he referred to as "muckers." Rutgers College in New Brunswick supplied many of the laboratory workers.

Edison continued to rely on many foreign-born specialists, especially Germans and Englishmen. The large German communities in Newark and New York City were a reservoir of talent. Besides England-born Batchelor, Insull, and Kennelly, Edison hired Alfred O. Tate, who replaced Insull as his secretary and also became a business manager. Critics liked to believe that Edison hired foreign-born workers in order to pay paltry wages, but more likely his good experience with his original "boys"— several foreign-born—influenced his decision. Not that Edison was above some labor exploitation. Typical of the era, he often employed child laborers for menial tasks.

While Edison would not admit it, managing such a large and complex operation required that he adapt to the new environment along with his staff. His basic strategy was an extension of his previous experience, insofar as he intended to develop several products simultaneously to insure momentum in the lab and spread more thinly the risk of failure. However, it often kept the talented inventor from giving sufficient time to each project.

His informal style of management contrasted sharply with other leading businessmen, but it should not be confused with laxity. While he joked with his men and refused to remain aloof, he demanded hard work—and results. He was loath to pay his people any more than he could get away with, which he considered good business practice. But he also believed that employment in his lab was a form of compensation that no salary could match. On some occasions, when the work was particularly productive, he shared profits with his most trusted employees. Nevertheless, in Edison's mind, the success of any project superseded the practical interests of his staff. As a man who considered wealth an opportunity for more worthwhile tasks and not for acquisitive ends, Edison had little time for anything but results.

There was a lack of rigid structure in the work environment but a keen interest in turning promising research into marketable products. It was not unusual for Edison to give his staff the general outline of what he wanted, then turn them loose to find the best method of achieving the goal. He often switched employees from one task to another if a promising line of investigation materialized. Some of the professionally trained personnel found the random methods, the lack of formal reports, and the irregular hours impossible and left West Orange. Others thrived in the largely unfettered atmosphere. Once an idea was translated into a practical model, Edison demanded an assessment of feasibility and production cost. Precise experimental records were essential, but formal laboratory reports were considered window dressing.

The primary goal of his enterprise at West Orange was practical and profitable inventions, the same goal he had been striving for throughout his professional life. But his direct participation in the daily experiments and in the exhilaration of discovery were being compromised by his growing list of managerial and administrative responsibilities, as well as the pressures of celebrity. He needed to go through his voluminous mail each morning, and he regularly met with the men in charge of key experiments in his library. Nevertheless, he routinely toured the laboratory, as he had done at Menlo Park, stopping to examine the progress at every station. His powers of observation and his retention of myriad details made these visits more than perfunctory exercises. He rarely had time to devote to any one line of inquiry, although he periodically allowed himself the luxury of jumping into a project when something special caught his attention.

The scale of his operation increasingly forced him to support—rather than control—the work of his staff; and growing competition in the marketplace compelled him to rely on the opinion of specialists. It was no secret that he did not work well with independently minded individuals, often ignoring them, allowing them to founder, and sometimes driving them off. His personal style of management was not always suited to his goals. The size of the West Orange laboratory could be as much a barrier as an aid to innovation.

Not surprisingly, modern industrial laboratories sought more systematic methods of research and development. Certainly, few individuals possessed the unique skills of the great inventor to emulate his approach. But the models for the modern industrial laboratory, the General Electric industrial laboratory (1900) and the Bell Laboratory (1911) in particular, had narrower interests than Edison. They sought to sustain control over their respective industries through research and development. Most industrial research outside of the electrical power and communications fields, however, emphasized testing. The need for basic scientific research at West Orange was secondary to testing, in an environment where the emphasis was on the development and manufacture of consumable goods.

Edison's lab was the nerve center of his manufacturing. But both Menlo Park and West Orange contributed in a general rather than a specific way to the evolution of industrial research and development. Edison taught industries about team research and about the need to seek outside funding. Most important, he demonstrated that "there was money to be made in the development and control of advanced technologies." If West Orange was not an archetype for modern industrial research and development, it was a testament to the marketing of invention.

Although Edison first sold his inventions to business moguls, as an independent businessman he rarely lost sight of the value of his urban marketplace and the wealth of potential consumers. He kept a constant eye on lowering manufacturing costs. Spending time and money on inventions with little market appeal or devoting energies to pioneering products was, in most cases, foreign to his thinking. However, he was not opposed to basic scientific research in his laboratories—if it had commercial potential or broader applications. Edison began nearly all his project with a market analysis, including data on potential consumers, the current status of the technology, and the activities of competitors. The development of the incandescent lighting system and the phonograph probably gave him his greatest initial experience in marketing discrete, but widely successful, technologies. The lessons learned in the 1870s and 1880s were applied again and again into the twentieth century.

Funding his activities remained a chronic concern. A large part of the fortune he made in electric lighting went to pay for building West Orange, related business activities, and his new house. He wanted to move beyond using his own money to pay the gigantic costs of this facility, especially operating expenses of the lab—$80,000 a year—and the cost of research and testing. As a matter of course, he began to form "manufacturing shops" as soon as experimental projects became commercially viable. These organizations were billed for the development work on the product and then became permanent customers for the laboratory. The manufacturing shops provided Edison with a steady income and plenty of business.

This procedure alone did not insure financial success. Edison remained dependent on venture capitalists to supply funds for experimentation, testing, and development to help support the cost of manufacturing and establishing markets and to share the financial risk of unsuccessful products. West Orange also accumulated funds through contract research and manufacturing and repair activities. In the 1890s, especially, Edison General Electric underwrote a substantial portion of the experimental work at West Orange because of the heavy emphasis on electrical projects. The laboratory devoted considerable energy to reducing the cost of incandescent lamps.

The West Orange facility did not exude the romance of the little Menlo Park research center, but neither did it detract from Edison's image as a great inventor. By 1889 West Orange was carrying on more than seventy experimental projects (possibly more than could have been handled effectively), staggering in breadth and range. This was the site where Edison and his staff continued work on the electric lighting system, where the phonograph was perfected, where the motion picture camera and the dictating machine were invented, and where the storage battery was developed.

Experimentation and testing in the electrical field were central. However, since Edison tenaciously defended DC power at the time, and was fighting off Westinghouse and other advocates of AC power, that research took few new turns. Not so in the case of the phonograph. The establishment of the Edison Phonograph Works in May 1888 rounded out the original plan for West Orange. With the completion of the electric light system, Edison returned to the phonograph, intending to make it a commercial success. While the phonograph had brought Edison great notoriety in the early years, it had yet to provide much income. Profitability became an obsession, and Edison devoted considerable time to marketing his favorite brainchild throughout the world. He hoped that the phonograph and research in electricity would help to establish the financial base for other inventions. While phonograph sales in the beginning of the 1890s were a paltry $25,000 per year, they topped $250,000 per year by the turn of the century.

Competition in the field also brought Edison back to the phonograph. As Bell's invention of the telephone drew Edison's attention, so Edison's phonograph attracted Bell. "It is a most astonishing thing to me," Bell stated in an 1877 letter, "that I could possibly have let this invention slip through my fingers when I consider how my thoughts have been directed to this subject for so many years past." Realizing that much remained to be done with the wondrous new discovery, Alexander Bell's cousin, Chichester Bell, and instrument maker Charles Sumner Tainter developed a prototype at the Volta Associates Laboratory in Washington. In 1885 they applied for a patent on their "graphophone." Based largely on Edison's design, the new machine was electrically driven, mounted with a floating stylus, and utilized waxed cardboard instead of tinfoil for the recording surface.

Representatives of Bell and Tainter approached Edison privately in 1886 with the proposition that they jointly market an improved phonograph. Edison, his baby ready to be snatched from his arms, was furious and refused to enter into an agreement with this "bunch of pirates." No matter that he had ignored the invention for a decade; in his eyes the phonograph was his claim to originality.

"Shocked into action," Edison began new research on the phonograph in 1887, shortly before his move to West Orange. By then, however, many in his original research team had scattered or had been reassigned; some had died. His old friend and matchmaker, Ezra T. Gilliland, left his job at Bell Telephone's Mechanical Department and helped to conduct new experiments. By 1888 much of the work in the lab switched to research on the basic phonograph, including various commercial uses such as a coin-operated amusement phonograph, a clockwork phonograph, and a talking doll.

Edison apparently borrowed the idea of the floating stylus from the "pirates" and wrestled with the problem of sound reproduction. He also began studying how to duplicate cylinders in larger numbers. In the spring of 1888, a much-awaited demonstration of his new machine for potential backers flopped because of a glitch in replacing the old reproducing stylus, thus squelching an opportunity to pick up financial support. Soon, however, Edison was ready to do battle in a phonographic war, as he had done with the telephone and the telegraph.

In a deal with Pittsburgh millionaire Jesse W. Lippincott, who previously had acquired the Bell/Tainter graphophone patent, Edison sold his rights but retained the power to manufacture the machine, thus obtaining capital and avoiding a costly court battle. Lippincott formed the North American Phonograph Company intending to produce a commercial dictating machine to be leased to businesses. Yet the project also handsomely lined the pockets of Gilliland and John Tomlinson, Edison's attorney. The affair may have been a breach of ethics rather than fraud, but Edison had been duped. He would not be so trusting of confederates in the future.

But he still had his phonograph business. At his new West Orange laboratory, Edison erected a large factory and research facilities. The continuing war, however, was not so much fought over who could build the better mousetrap as over marketing, especially the use of the machine as a music box. Its entertainment value was demonstrated by showmen who attracted crowds to pay for the privilege of listening to the machine.

Edison did not like this turn of events. "I don't want the phonograph sold for amusement purposes," he protested. "It is not a toy. I want it sold for business purposes only." But he had little choice but to join in the race if he wanted to maintain his share of the market. He responded by manufacturing coin-operated machines placed in penny arcades in several large cities. He then turned to the home market, improving the fidelity of the machine and designing attractive wooden cabinets. The growing mass market also demanded the application of mass production techniques, but it took several years before the West Orange facility could meet its targets.

Edison continued to perfect the phonograph. The 1889–1890 model combined a recorder with reproducer in one instrument, which made it potentially valuable as a home entertainment device, but additional work on a new cylinder and stylus required two more years before marketing. The recording capability, however, was sub-standard for an Edison product. In 1890 he started several experimental projects to recreate the sound of music. With Walter Miller, he developed an automatic reproducer for the new models in 1893 which was a major step in meeting the goal. The use of a jeweled—instead of steel—stylus was a key innovation in the design, but the harder stylus required a harder wax on the cylinder. Jonas Aylsworth worked diligently to find such a compound. By 1894 Edison was convinced that his new phonograph reproduced music "almost perfectly" and would lead to a commercial grade amusement phonograph. Marketing the machines then became a top priority.

A dependable power source also posed problems. Edison tried several approaches, including a battery and electric motor combination, a spring motor, a treadle, a house-current motor, and even a water motor—none completely satisfactory. But he kept searching.

For a time, Edison demonstrated a reticence to produce phonographs with a spring motor. In 1894 he developed a new, lighter, electric motor, but the spring-motor machines of other manufacturers were attracting consumers. Emile Berliner brought out a "hear gramophone" that used a spring motor. While the machine could only reproduce and not record, it was perfect for the music market where a cheaper and simpler machine met the needs of most Americans. Columbia Phonograph Company and American Graphophone Company introduced spring-motor machines selling for as little as ten or twenty dollars. Edison viewed these machines as toys with limited capabilities, not the high-quality machines he believed he was building. In 1896, however, Edison moved into the spring-motor market with a forty-dollar machine, and purchases skyrocketed. By 1903 sales figures passed the one-million-dollar mark for the first time.

The sales of the spring-motor phonographs set off a greater demand for records. Edison's invention of gold-plating masters for mass-producing records in 1900 transformed the business. Competition now moved beyond the equipment to capturing the public's music tastes. Edison had long preferred catering to the common man. But he found himself having to break into the middle and "high brow" markets, compelled to attract operatic stars and other new artists to his stable of recording entertainers. The Edison company also tried to win more specialized markets, such as music for foreign-born city dwellers, and music for rural Americans. Advertising campaigns in the early 1900s reflected the efforts to target special audiences: "On the farm and on the ranch, more than anywhere else, does the Edison phonograph prove itself a blessing." "If you are a good-natured and a shrewd farmer you will see that your farm hands get some of the benefits of the phonograph."

Sales of cylinder phonographs began to slip markedly after 1907, due in large measure to the growing success of the disc record. In 1887, Emile Berliner developed a system that made practical the use of flat records rather than cylinders. After that, marketing claims focused on the comparative advantages and disadvantages of the cylinder versus the disc—which could play longer, had better fidelity, was better quality, and was cheaper. Columbia and Victor now had entered the field, and by the turn of the century, newly established European competitors such as Gramophone Company in England and Pathé in France utilized the flat disc.

In 1906 Victor Talking Machine Company introduced the Victrola, a disc machine aimed at the middle and high end of the market. While the original disc machines were manufactured cheaply to attract consumers of modest means, the Victrola posed a direct competitive threat to Edison who had stressed quality over price. To meet the challenge, the Edison laboratory fabricated a new cylinder machine in 1908, the Amberola, designed to play the four-minute Amberol cylinder. With the introduction of the superior Blue Amberol records in 1912, the Amberola became a popular addition to the Edison line. But it gave the Victrola little competition, especially in the affluent urban markets where the disc machine enjoyed a tremendous following.

Dividing the market was a temporary solution at best. For example, with Edison only manufacturing cylinders and Victor only manufacturing discs, a cooperative approach to marketing seemed possible. Victor eventually sold its line through Edison dealers, but quickly siphoned much of the business previously dominated by the cylinder machines. Edison soon grew angry with Victor—"that Vic bunch of incompetents and fakers"—as with other competitors. He counterattacked with new marketing strategies, emphasizing the value of the Edison name on quality products. At one point, Edison recommended that home demonstration of his phonographs be targeted to large cities where Victor was strong. "We must as soon as possible adopt a scheme to get more Amberolas in homes. If we wait too long the Victrola will be so preponderating that we never can gain a position in the field."

With the erosion of the split market, and after various stopgap measures to improve the cylinders, Edison was forced to develop his own disc-playing machine. While Edison continued experimental work on the Amberola and the Blue Amberol record, he introduced a disc phonograph in 1913. Two years later a whole line of disc machines were placed on the market. However, the failure to produce a successful low-priced disc machine limited his customers to the more affluent—a result that certainly went against his marketing philosophy for the cylinder and other consumer products.

Edison sometimes followed rather than led in the race to capture the music box market in the late nineteenth and early twentieth centuries. His application of the phonograph to the urban business world, however, was pioneering. The cylinder machine adapted well to the development of dictating equipment, especially since his phonographs could record as well as reproduce sound. Edison's business dictating machine—the Ediphone—recorded the voice as spoken into the receiver and captured it on the wax cylinder. Completed cylinders went to the secretary who listened to them on a Secretarial Ediphone and transcribed the message with a typewriter. An electric key provided start, stop, and repeat control from the typewriter keyboard. As the ads stated, the secretary had "the voice at her fingertips." Edison's staff aggressively marketed this equipment, promoting it as a convenient device for office and home. "An Ediphone at a man's desk tells the world he values his time!"

He also fathered several other inventions for the business world. The telescribe, coupling a telephone and a phonograph, recorded conversations automatically. After a demonstration of the phonograph in Berlin, German chancellor Otto von Bismarck proposed that concealed phonographs might be used to secretly record diplomatic conversations.

While Edison devoted considerable time at West Orange to mass communications—not only the phonograph, but motion pictures as well—his interest in industrial production also grew. His preoccupation with an elaborate ore-milling process (which concentrated low-grade magnetic iron ore—magnetite—into compact briquettes) was once considered "Edison's Folly." He believed that ore milling had the potential to transform the production of iron and steel in the United States and would provide cheap iron ore to the declining blast furnaces of the Northeast. This project, into which he sank an enormous portion of his personal fortune, now appears to be a logical extension of his growing interest in manufacturing and industrial production in the 1880s.

Edison had come to appreciate the connection between invention and production by the time the lighting system was completed. The range and scale of his inventive activities had grown immeasurably as did his emphasis on systems and networks, especially those that connected a technology to its market. Having the financial wherewithal in the 1880s, he could think bigger, act bigger, and ultimately practice the economies of scale essential to the success of the Rockefellers, Carnegies, and other business magnates of the day.

A major commitment to expanding his electrical system and participating more aggressively in electrical power development seemed to be the most logical direction for Edison. However, the commitment to DC power painted him into a corner, at least temporarily. And the extent and nature of his competition gave Edison little maneuvering room. Ore milling, to the contrary, was a wide-open field with many inventive possibilities, which also suited Edison's growing interest as an industrialist.

Edison slipped into the ore-separation work through a back door. During the course of developing his electric light system at Menlo Park in 1879, he searched for available sources of platinum as filament material. Before he focused on carbonized thread, platinum seemed to offer the greatest potential for a long-lived filament. The metal was relatively scarce, however, and thus would be expensive to employ in the lamps. One solution was extracting platinum for various ores. This approach failed to produce the desired results, but Edison continued to tinker with extracting other metals—gold, silver, lead, tin—and ended up inventing a magnetic separator for iron ore, receiving his first patents in 1880.

Immediately he formed a new business, the Edison Ore-Milling Company, bent on exploiting his invention. In the summer of 1881 he set up two plants on the beaches of Quogue, Long Island and Quonocontaug, Rhode Island to remove iron from the black magnetic sand. He then informed the press that his next step was to search the entire United States coastline for additional plant sites. But the project never lived up to Edison's enthusiasm. One vessel loaded with ore was driven onto the rocks; another started to sink after being loaded. Worst of all, in September 1882 a storm rumbled in and washed the beaches clean of its black sand.

More significant than the intervention of nature was Edison's disregard for his cardinal rule of invention: Find a market before starting a new venture. He had given little thought initially to who would buy his processed ore. Storm or no storm, without customers the ore-milling process was no more than an interesting technical problem.

Edison did not return to ore milling until 1887. By that time several conditions had changed. The establishment of General Electric brought Edison considerable financial resources which he was willing to use as working capital for a new venture. Competition in the electrical power field and the establishment of the West Orange facilities focused his attention more fully on new industrial enterprises. Edison once again began to consider the technical and economic prospects of the ore-milling operation.

The iron mines of the East Coast had become virtually exhausted. They were not capable of competing with the rich mines of Michigan and the West, which were also more technically sophisticated and better managed. But as the need for iron ore continued to be felt in the East, it was irksome to pay the heavy transport costs to bring the ore from northern Michigan. By applying his magnetic process to the tired mines of the East, Edison hoped to develop a worthy competitor to the western mines. While the idea made economic sense, implementation was another matter. Edison believed he could overcome the economic risks with sufficient attention to the efficiency and scale of his technical system. The triumph of technology over economics—just the type of delicious problem that Edison could not resist.

In January 1889 Edison formed New Jersey and Pennsylvania Concentrating Works, and began a survey of available sites for his magnetic separation process. Aside from production of iron ore, he also planned to construct separators, license them to mining companies, and sell territorial rights throughout the United States. Failing to attract needed investors, Edison decided to run his own mines first and then negotiate directly with other mine owners to promote his new technology.

Direct involvement in the new industrial enterprise soon consumed him. A pilot plant established at Bechtelville, Pennsylvania in mid-1889, convinced the Wizard that potentially huge profits were available in the field. He became "intoxicated" with the profit potential. A plant near Ogdensburg, New Jersey, followed, and it became the center of operations for the ore-separation venture. Only sixty miles from Newark, the site was close enough to West Orange for Edison to keep an eye on his other interests, and remote enough for him to avoid returning if he became absorbed in ore milling.

Search parties with magnetic-needle devices had been mapping deposits all along the Appalachian Mountains. They found the promising site at Ogdensburg on the New Jersey-Pennsylvania border, where Edison bought sixteen thousand acres dotted with abandoned mines. Edison spent five years in the dreary highlands of New Jersey. Mina reconciled herself to Tom's long absences and realized the honeymoon was truly over. "I'm luckier than many wives," she said. "At least I know where my husband is."

The village of Ogden became the industrial village of "Edison," but was hardly less primitive and lacking in creature comforts. Coldwater shacks, primitive plumbing, and few diversions marked life on Sparta Mountain. Nonetheless, optimism was high. At its peak, Edison employed about four hundred workers at the site. Two experts, John Birkinbine (a prominent Philadelphia mining engineer) and Walter S. Mallory (a Chicago iron manufacturer) consulted on the project. Mallory became plant superintendent at Ogdensburg, having served as a chief official in the Upper Pennsylvania enterprise as well. Some questioned his administrative ability, but he and Edison hit it off well and worked closely together throughout the venture.

Some of Edison's stalwarts, especially Batchelor and Upton, also participated in the project. By and large, Edison made the executive decisions, especially in marketing the iron ore. Birkinbine, who was possibly the most knowledgeable consultant, was fired just as the plant was beginning to operate. Success of the operation clearly rested on the shoulders of the "Old Man."

The great strength of the venture was Edison's know-how in devising a sophisticated technical system of ore separation. Although magnetic processes had been used before, Edison adapted them for large-scale operation (although it was a very expensive process at best). The custom-made facility utilized large traveling cranes, and later gigantic steam shovels that stripped the rock from the ore seam and deposited it onto a cableway or railroad skip to be carried to the plant. An amazing system of conveyor belts for moving the material along, giant rollers and grinders for reducing the stones as large as five or six tons to fine powder, and large magnets for deflecting the iron ore completed the process.

At first Edison tried shipping the ore in bulk, but it proved too fine to stay in place. As an alternative, he made porous cakes out of the ore and baked them into briquettes. Henry Ford, who became great friends with Edison in the 1920s, recalled reading articles on Edison's ore-mining operation. Apparently the process influenced the first "beltline" system for the Model-T automobile. Years after the plant closed, Ford remarked that the Ogden project encompassed the most complete automatic conveyor system up to that time.

Despite the fact that there were many breakdowns and several accidents—Edison himself got buried with rubble while trying to fix a cranky piece of machinery—technical problems did not undermine the success of the project. Marketability of the briquettes and timing were the twin demons. Edison counted on accessibility to eastern blast furnaces and cheaper freight costs to make his venture go. Efficient operation, he believed, would insulate the plant from even significant drops in the price of iron. He calculated that his concentrate could be shipped for

$2.32 per ton as opposed to $3.00 per ton, which was the average freight cost of ore from Michigan and Minnesota. Most important was volume production, and Edison wanted to process five thousand tons daily—four times the capacity of existing plants.

Taking his ideas from the drawing board to the plant site was another matter. Since Edison did not depend on outside capital for the venture, and had few top-flight advisers to present alternative views, he did not consider all the potential roadblocks. Despite some promising tests of the briquettes and a big order from Bethlehem Steel, by the time he was ready for full production in 1899 the bottom fell out of the market.

When he began his enterprise, a comparable quality of iron ore delivered at Pittsburgh was fetching $4.25 to $7.50 per ton. In 1891 Edison delivered Ogden concentrate for $4.75, well within competitive limits. By the time he was in a position to take large orders, the price had fallen to $3.90 and then to $2.25. But the drop in price was only one of several problems. The Panic of 1893, which devastated many businesses, ravaged potential markets and weakened the national economy. Huge, pure deposits of iron ore discovered in the Mesabi Range in Minnesota in 1890 began pouring into the eastern markets by 1892. This undermined Edison's careful calculation of the competing supplies of iron ore. In addition, the locks of Sault Sainte Marie Canal—connecting Lake Superior to Lake Huron—were expanded, allowing larger ships to pass through and thus further depressing the landed price of ore in the East.

Even if prices remained stable, the quality of the concentrate never lived up to expectations. The phosphorous content was much too high, despite major efforts to reduce it. Some questioned the performance of the briquettes in the blast furnace. But Edison argued that the briquettes would require less fuel and consequently less labor in the conversion process. Blast furnace operators, however, preferred more familiar ores rather than take a chance on a speculation, even Edison's speculation. Without other considerations, the cost of production alone demanded that the Ogden plant process ten thousand tons per day, which was a Herculean undertaking even for the Wizard.

"Well, it's all gone, but we had a hell of a good time spending it!" This purportedly was Edison's summary of the financial drag of the bust venture on his bank account. In eleven years, he had invested more than three million dollars in the ore separation business, two-thirds of which was his own funds. He had borrowed money from everyone, even Batchelor and Upton. He had mortgaged the Phonograph Works and cut back on West Orange operations. And he had liquidated all his General Electric stock. The $175,000 he raised from dismantling the plant went to pay off the company's bills, not to reduce his personal debt. Few could see much humor in his claim that a seventy-five-dollar-a-month telegraph operator job was always waiting for him.

The ore-separation venture says a great deal about Edison as an inventor and businessman. The project, at least in the beginning, was not simply "Edison's Folly." After an initial lapse, he saw a market to supply and mustered his inventive skills to lick the technical problems of turning low-grade ore into high-grade concentrate. But he lost sight of the economic limits by placing too much faith in his technical skills to overcome increasingly ominous signs of a deteriorating market. He also let his work slide at West Orange, resulting in a sharp reduction in the output of other inventions.

However, the venture demonstrated an extraordinary trait in Edison—resilience. The downside of that quality was stubbornness and intolerance for the ideas of others. On the positive side, Edison shucked off defeat about as well as anyone could. In the wake of his doomed ore-separation venture, he not only found the will to continue with the rest of his work, but insisted on finding ways of turning his ore-milling disaster into a belated success. Amazingly in 1897 he fostered the establishment of Edison Ore Milling Syndicate in England, a perfect example of his "never-say-die" attitude. In addition, he also became aware of a by-product of the ore-milling venture—cement—for which he believed he could develop a new market.

Turning failures into successes often depended upon a return to urban markets, where his most productive endeavors bore fruit. Not long after the closing of the Ogden plant, Edison founded the Edison Portland Cement Company in June 1899. The techniques learned in ore milling could immediately be put to use in the production of cement, and after a period of testing, Edison established a mechanized plant ready for operation in 1902. He also bought a large tract of limestone-bearing land near Stewartsville in western New Jersey, near the center of the nation's cement industry. This was another expensive venture that depended on high volume. But faith in Edison's abilities had not been irreparably damaged, and his powers of persuasion had not faded. By 1905 the total investment in the operation topped three million dollars, raised from many of the same individuals involved in the ore-milling deal. A promotional brochure, "The Facts About Edison Cement," made the following claim: "When a company has a reputation for radical and successful departure from established methods of manufacture, any changes in its plant rouse general interest. The Edison Portland Cement Company has such a reputation."

Edison focused on scale of operations and technical superiority to compete in what he rightly perceived as a growth industry. Fortunately some of the finest deposits of limestone and cement rock in the United States were only a few miles from Edison's old iron mine. He developed a huge roasting kiln that increased output by 400 percent over conventional kilns, and he developed a grinding process that produced the most finely ground and precisely mixed product on the market. By World War I, the new company was the fifth largest producer in the United States. Some 180,000 bags of Edison Portland Cement went into the building of Yankee Stadium. Throughout the country Edison's cement was employed in the construction of hotels, factories, schools, dams, highways, bridges, and tunnels. In Havana, Cuba, it was used in large apartment complexes.

Edison was not satisfied simply to produce Portland Cement. He began to envision new uses for the product. He campaigned for mass-produced poured concrete homes, cheap enough for every workingman and his family in the country, fire resistant and sanitary. He developed complete sets of reusable metal moulds that would allow a builder to pour the concrete for the house in six hours and have a completely fabricated home ready for occupancy within two weeks—including the time it took for the cement to dry. "We will give the working man and his family ornamentation in their home," Edison stated. "They deserve it, and besides, it costs no more after the pattern is made to give decorative effects than it would to make everything plain." For an estimated twelve hundred dollars, plus the cost of the lot, the Edison concrete house would have four bedrooms, a parlor, a living room, a kitchen and bath, plus front and back porches.

The idea seemed too good to be true. A house for twelve hundred dollars! A new cut stone house sold for thirty thousand dollars. It was an idea that people wanted to believe in. A story in the May 19, 1908 issue of *Phoenix Gazette* noted that the well-insulated concrete house "is beyond a doubt a good example of what the average American home will be in a few years from now, when both wood and coal have become too expensive." Some people were understandably skeptical: "This idea is one of the insanities of genius. Edison is crazy. He wouldn't be a great inventor if he were not."

Although the process was technically feasible, it was economically impractical. Builders would have to invest at least $175,000 in moulds and equipment, which might be possible in an era of tract homes and major developers, but almost impossible in an era of small contractors with limited resources. Decades later it was resurrected as a way of building cheap housing in New York slums and as a precedent for prefabricated single-family dwellings. While Edison had identified a potentially deep market, the timing was wrong.

Edison did not stop with concrete houses. He also envisioned other uses for his cement—concrete furniture, concrete refrigerators, concrete phonograph cabinets, concrete pianos, concrete tombstones. "I am going to put concrete furniture on the market in the near future that will make it possible for a laboring man to put into his home furniture more artistic and more durable than is now to be found in the most palatial residences in Paris or along the Rhine," he claimed. "It will be cheap. If I couldn't put out my concrete furniture cheaper than oak that comes from Grand Rapids, I wouldn't go into the business." But this unusual product line met with predictable skepticism. Various commentators had great fun at Edison's expense. One cartoonist showed parents peering into a room where their young son was beating on a concrete piano with a hammer. The mother says to the father, "Just see him pound the new piano!"

It is sometimes difficult to discern the innovator from the hyperbole of the promoter/huckster. It is also difficult to determine where Edison was seeking new markets and where he was trying to create demand. In the case of the Portland Cement venture, Edison was able to nurse the company through several reorganizations and bankruptcies to survive until 1930. In the case of his concrete houses and furniture, he had struck a chord for low-cost housing and furnishings for an urban market, even though he received healthy chiding in the press. While the ventures had little chance for immediate commercial success, they pointed in the direction Edison's inventive interests were moving, that is, toward a mass market eager for new—and sometimes exotic—products. More dramatic would be the work in the field of mass communications, especially with his improved phonograph and his Kinetoscope, where revolutionary changes in entertainment and education awaited the explosion of new inventions.

CHAPTER EIGHT

The Persistence of Vision

The 1893 Chicago World's Fair was a smashing success. It was the largest of numerous fairs held in the late nineteenth century and triumphantly advertised Chicago's recovery and progress since the devastating fire of 1871. It also showcased innumerable exhibits of agricultural and industrial technology, and its life-sized model of the ideal city—the "White City"—promoted the City Beautiful Movement, which merged landscaping with architecture and engineering in an effort to enhance civic design. Architectural modernist Louis Sullivan ridiculed the excesses of the White City. "Architecture," he said, "died in the land of the free and the home of the brave. . . ." But twenty-seven million visitors flocked to Chicago nevertheless to gape at the new gadgets, to ride the rides on the midway, and to escape their daily routines.

Ironically, in a year that celebrated the material achievements and ingenuity of the world's artisans, inventors, and businessmen, the nation plunged into a depression that underscored the faltering industrial system. In mid-February, alarm suddenly hit the stock market when one million shares in the Philadelphia and Reading Railroad were quickly dumped, leaving the company bankrupt. Investors' fears continued to rack the stock market, with May 5 recording the worst day until the crash of 1929.

The Panic of 1893 lasted until late in the decade. Investment dropped sharply, thousands of businesses failed, banks (especially in New York) were pummeled, and factories and mines shut down. At its height, approximately three million people lost their jobs. "I have seen more misery in this last week," a Chicago journalist lamented, "than I ever saw in my life before."

Many businessmen blamed the Democratic administration of Grover Cleveland, who also became a casualty of the financial disaster. But the roots of the depression were much deeper, attributable to an overextended economy that placed too much faith in unending growth. From farms to factories the misery was widespread with breadlines, soup kitchens, and millions of disgruntled and disillusioned Americans. As Henry Adams recalled about the state of affairs in New England, "Men died like flies under the strain, and Boston grew suddenly old, haggard, and thin."

The currents of 1893 caught Thomas Edison as well. Because of the Panic, he laid off two hundred forty employees of the Edison Phonograph Works, and several of his other business ventures struggled throughout the decade. Even the spectacle of the Chicago World's Fair failed to offer much of a showcase for West Orange inventions. But in 1893 Edison experienced satisfying moments as well as painful lows. In that year he entered the field of motion pictures, the newest and potentially most revolutionary form of mass entertainment yet devised. In February he opened the Kinetographic Theater—the first American studio to produce motion pictures—and he also began to manufacture the Kinetoscope, the device for viewing them.

The new enterprise was a stepchild of Edison's interest in the phonograph. His involvement in motion pictures was more derivative, more typical of other projects where he perfected an existing technology or product and exploited its emerging market. In this case, Edison went further than before in claiming the superiority of his innovations, in minimizing the contributions of subordinates, and in dealing ruthlessly with competitors. As a result, few were willing to credit him with the invention of motion pictures. His image as a struggling inventor had been long since replaced by his reputation as a mainstay in the American business establishment. Edison was the first to commercialize motion pictures—a substantial achievement—but had little grounds on which to claim more.

The mechanical development of motion pictures was the end result of several converging technologies from Europe and the United States. In 1834 English mathematician William George Horner created a zoetrope, or "wheel of life," a circular drum with vertical slits that held a paper strip covered with drawings. When this stroboscopic machine twirled, objects on the strip appeared to be moving. "The persistence of vision," in which images lingered in the eye for a split second after they are removed from view, was the principle of optics that allowed these toys (and the machines that followed) to produce a sense of motion.

In the same year, Austrian artillery officer and teacher Baron Franz von Uchatius combined a stroboscopic toy with a "magic lantern" (similar to a slide projector) to create the Projecting Phenakistiscope, a device that threw off sequential animated movements when the lantern shone through a spinning slitted disk. Hundreds of variations of these toys existed by the end of the nineteenth century.

Experiments in photography offered a complementary avenue for developing motion pictures. The first attempts at motion photography were posed stills that simulated continuous action. Eadweard Muybridge, an Englishman living in California, was the first to separate a single process of motion into its component parts using photography. An itinerant photographer and inventor, Muybridge had a scandalous past due to a messy divorce and the murder of his wife's lover. His photographic expertise caught the attention of Leland Stanford, governor of California and former railroad magnate, who hired him in 1872 to help settle a twenty-five thousand dollar bet. An avid horse breeder and racer, the governor had wagered with a friend that, while running, all four hooves of a horse leave the ground at the same time.

Muybridge worked for five years to provide Stanford with the irrefutable evidence to win his bet. (Although it cost Stanford one hundred thousand dollars in expenses to do it!) The photographer lined up several cameras along the race track; each camera was fitted with a wire stretched across the track. As the horse galloped, it tripped the wires and thus released each camera shutter. The resulting photographs revealed that all the horse's hooves indeed left the ground at once.

Stanford's satisfaction was less important than the boost to motion photography. For the next twenty years, Muybridge perfected his multiple-camera technique, using more cameras and an array of subjects from elephants to nude women. His new experiments, however, did not appreciably advance his initial contribution. While he successfully divided continuous motion into distinct frames, no one had photographed the sequence with a single camera.

Etienne-Jules Marey took the crucial step toward developing a film camera. The French physiologist shot the first motion pictures with a single camera in 1882. His invention looked like a shotgun, using a long barrel for its lens and a circular chamber containing a single glass photographic plate. The plate circulated twelve times per second and permitted twelve exposures. Eventually he replaced the glass plate with paper roll firm. The convergence of several key experiments rapidly led to the modern motion picture camera and projector.

In the 1890s the curiosity with motion pictures passed from the world of science to the business world and into the marketplace, where Edison stepped in as the first with a commercial motion picture machine. Edison entered the motion picture business almost casually, without a clear sense of what he hoped to accomplish. His initial goal was finding a way to unite the phonograph with projected photos. He intended to enhance the value of the phonograph, not create a new mass medium. Asked by an interviewer what inspired the idea of the motion picture camera, Edison replied, "The phonograph. I had been working for several years on my experiments for recording and reproducing sound, and the thought occurred to me that it should be possible to devise an apparatus to do for the eye what the phonograph was designed to do for the ear."

In 1888 Edison had met Muybridge at West Orange and discussed uniting the phonograph with the motion photographer's zoopraxiscope. But Edison had no interest in collaborating with Muybridge. Instead he purchased a set of ninety plates, depicting various forms of motion, and assigned them to William K. L. Dickson, instructing the young assistant to develop a machine to project the images.

Long intrigued with photography, Edison had an extensive personal collection of stereopticons, viewers for three-dimensional pictures. He also acquired equipment and plates and incorporated darkrooms into both the Menlo Park and West Orange laboratories. He authorized a few minor photographic experiments during the mid-1880s. In Dickson, an amateur photographer himself, Edison had an enthusiastic colleague, who split his time between this fascinating new project and his duties as chief of the metallurgical laboratory for the ore-milling operation.

The initial design for the synchronized sight and sound machine borrowed directly from phonograph technology. Dickson placed tiny pictures taken on some sensitized material onto a cylinder. While the cylinder turned, light emanating from within projected the images outward. This proved unsuccessful, and Dickson sought alternatives to the cylinder concept. Synchronization of sight and sound also proved to be a major stumbling block at this time.

In 1889 a film shed was constructed next to Building 4, and Dickson—with the aid of an assistant—worked behind closed doors in Room 5 of the main laboratory. Dickson replaced the revolving cylinder with a celluloid strip. Celluloid film was first used in the 1880s with the experiments of John Carbutt of Philadelphia, the pioneer in dry plate making, and George Eastman of Rochester, the inventor of the "Kodak."

Eastman's celluloid film—thinner and more flexible than Carbutt's—covered with photographic emulsion, helped take the project in a new direction. Dickson added perforations to the edge of the strip to make it easier for the film to pass through the projecting device, a major breakthrough in the success of the motion picture camera and projector. "That's it," Edison exclaimed. "We've got it. Now work like hell." Dickson sent his first order to Eastman in 1889. Edison later noted that "Without George Eastman I don't know what the result would have been in the history of the motion picture."

The use of perforated film had to be matched with the development of practical film projection. Marey is credited with creating the first projector to use celluloid film on an endless belt, although it lacked a reliable mechanism to move the film past the lens. Other claims abound, but Edison was able to get to the market first with a commercial machine.

Upon returning from the Paris Exposition in October 1889, Edison was greeted by Dickson with a "Kinetophonograph" (*kinesis* is the Greek word for motion), which projected pictures on a screen and, in principle at least, was synchronized with sound. The faint image projected by Dickson's new device spoke out: "Good morning, Mr. Edison, glad to see you back. I hope that you are satisfied with the Kinetophonograph." While impressed, Edison rejected the device because the quality of the sound reproduction was poor, and development work continued.

In 1891 Edison filed patents for a "Kinetograph"—for taking pictures—and a "Kinetoscope"—for viewing. The Kinetograph was the manufacturing component used to make the films. Unlike modern cameras, it was a stationary device housed in a large box attached to a cast-iron base and driven by an electric motor. It was the most original part of Edison's motion picture system.

The Kinetoscope was the first viewing technology Edison used commercially. It was modeled after the coin-in-slot phonograph and allowed only one person at a time to view the film. The Kinetoscope was a pine box with a hole in the top for viewing. The upper portion contained an electric motor, a shutter, and an incandescent lamp; the lower part held a fifty-foot loop of film that traveled over rollers. The electricity came from a primary battery.

Edison's decision to push ahead with a peepshow device rather than a projection system was "based partly on his integrity as an inventor and partly on his greed as a businessman." Edison wanted to maximize the profits of the invention by parcelling the new medium to the public through a tightly managed technology. Using his experience with the phonograph as a guide, he took advantage of the novelty value of moving pictures as a way of opening a new market. In addition, the peephole offered greater clarity than the projected image at this stage of development.

But in the early 1890s Edison was not in a position to place his Kinetoscope into production. Ore milling was draining his assets, the Phonograph Works was losing money, and he had several other projects to contend with. A. O. Tate, with two partners associated with the North American Phonograph Company, stepped forward to acquire Edison's concession to market the peephole device in the United States. (Edison retained the overseas rights.) They hoped to unveil the invention at the Chicago World's Fair but were unable to get the machines in time. However, Frank Gammon, secretary of the awards committee, and his wealthy brother-in-law Norman C. Raff joined the group and began supplying customers in 1894. The peephole viewers were placed side by side with phonographs in amusement parlors.

The first Kinetoscope parlor opened in Manhattan in April. For twenty-five cents admission, the customer passed along a row of the peephole machines that were switched on by attendants. To lower overhead and increase profits, Edison devised a nickel-in-slot attachment for each machine, and the attendants became expendable.

The Kinetoscopes—later referred to generically as Nickelodeons—were an instant sensation. After the first parlors in New York, others cropped up in Chicago, San Francisco, and Atlantic City and eventually in every major city across the country. The Kinetoscope Company also installed the machines in department stores, hotels, saloons, and public phonograph parlors.

Success depended not only upon wide distribution of the machines but on the production of new films. The public quickly tired of the early films and demanded fresh and unique ones. The opening of the Kinetographic Theater in February 1893, on the premises of the West Orange facility, introduced the first movie studio to the world. The building, approximately forty feet long and ten feet wide, was made of wood covered with black tar paper. It could move on a track to follow the sunlight and had a roof that could open. The interior was painted black for high contrast and included a set of rails on which the bulky camera was mounted, allowing it to be rolled forward and back within the building. The cost of this first movie studio was $637.67.

The "Black Maria" as it was called—then current slang for the police "paddy wagon," which it resembled—was the scene of hundreds of productions. Dickson was the first cameraman and director. The first film actor was Fred Ott, immortalized in "Fred Ott's Sneeze." The bulk of the films, however, focused on vaudeville acts, boxing matches, and simple curiosities—all of which suited Edison's own tastes. Performers, coaxed from Manhattan to the New Jersey studio, included stage actors, such as Joseph Jefferson, as well as celebrities like Annie Oakley and Buffalo Bill Cody. Most movies were thirty-five to forty seconds in duration, because the camera could only hold fifty feet of film. There was no time for story or plot development, only a single, uncomplicated event staged in a mock Chinese laundry or on a simulated vaudeville stage.

No sooner was the Black Maria completed when Dickson had a nervous breakdown and was sent to Fort Myers for a ten-week rest. Upon his return it was apparent that the young motion picture pioneer felt cramped by Edison's approach to the new business venture. Dickson disliked shooting the boxing matches that Edison enjoyed, preferring to concentrate on more artistic subjects. He particularly resented the intrusion of William Gilmore, the manager of the phonographic works, who was put in charge of the Kinetoscope business in 1894. But what rankled Dickson most was Edison's unwillingness to allow him to develop a projection system.

Norman Raff had approached Edison about developing a screen projection camera, but he shot back, "If we make this screen machine that you are asking for, it will spoil everything."

Unlike earlier situations—such as the debates over cylinder and disc records or DC and AC power—Edison was not stubbornly clinging to a familiar technology but was concentrating on immediate profits. "It was better not to kill the goose that laid the golden eggs," he argued. According to his calculations, the demand for projection equipment would be far less than for Kinetoscopes because so many more people could view a projected film. And from an experimental perspective, Edison was more interested in solving the problem of sight and sound synchronization than developing projection equipment.

This may have been a narrow business perspective but one that Dickson could not change. The productive relationship with Edison was coming to an end. Edison purportedly dismissed Dickson in 1894—on the advice of Gilmore—upon suspicion that he was planning to join a competitor. Dickson, however, simply may have been drawn to a new business venture to develop a projection system, an opportunity denied him by Edison.

By 1894 competition in the fledgling industry was beginning to heat up, and Edison was becoming less able to control its growth or its direction. This was particularly true because the novelty of the peepshow device was short-lived as the public clamored for more than a forty-second sideshow. Some within the Edison fold, including Raff, realized that projecting pictures would be the next step up from the Kinetoscope. Competitors, however, led the way toward the modern movie industry.

In Europe, Auguste Lumière and his brother Louis dabbled with Edison's equipment in 1894 and developed the Cinematographe—a portable camera and projector, distributed from France to Russia and the Far East. The Lumières opened their first theater in Paris in December 1895. They quickly became international leaders in the industry, not only developing a portable camera/projector but also standardizing film width at 35mm and film speed at sixteen frames per second (until the era of talkies). In fact, innovations came from all over Europe, including the work of Frenchman Louis Augustin Le Prince, William Friese-Greene and Robert W. Paul in England, and Max and Emil Skladanowski in Germany.

In the United States, the Latham family (who attracted Dickson) resolved an important technical problem associated with projection. The Lathams devised a simple method of dealing with intermittent movement, that is, the need to stop each frame for a fraction of a second to allow light to pass through the projector's lens. Such movement had a tendency to tear the films, especially long strips, as they passed through the projector. The "Latham loop" left slack in the film at the top and bottom of the film gate allowing for proper movement through the machine. The Lathams incorporated this idea into their camera and projection system developed in 1895 and doubled the width of the Edison film strip from 35mm to 70mm for a clearer picture.

The Lathams were a curious lot, a Virginia family of adventurers and inventors, part showmen, part businessmen. Major Woodville Latham was a former Confederate officer and chemistry instructor. His sons, Gray and Otway, also became involved in the motion picture business, but they took up the playboy life soon after arriving in New York.

In the summer of 1895 the upright Dickson, who disapproved of the conduct of the Lathams, left New York City and joined another group in Syracuse. Dickson claimed to have developed the Mutoscope in 1894, a mechanical flip-card device operated by a hand crank meant to be a direct competitor with the Kinetoscope. With mechanic and draftsman Herman Casler and another partner, Dickson established the KMCD Company, which evolved into the American Mutoscope Company. However, after marketing the new peepshow contraption, Dickson and his colleagues developed the much more significant Biograph, a projection machine, one of the key innovations that helped to turn the motion picture business in its modern direction.

The Biograph and other projection machines forced the hand of the Kinetoscope Company and led Edison into a curious relationship with Thomas Armat, a realtor from Washington, D.C. Armat—discovering the principle that film movement had to be intermittent—also developed a "loop" and designed a workable projector (with associate Charles F. Jenkins). Armat and Edison—through the intercession of Raff—entered into an agreement that had Edison selling the Armat projector under the name, Vitascope.

Newspapers hailed "Edison's latest marvel, the Vitascope." Of the premier on April 23, 1896, the *New York Times* proclaimed, "The views were all wonderfully real and singularly exhilarating." The deal with silent partner Armat was a shortcut that put Edison back into the middle of the hotly competitive motion picture market but had Edison relying on the power of his name rather than the strength of his own inventive abilities.

In 1895 Edison, along with the Lumières, still rode atop the new industry, but the competition was getting much stiffer and increasingly destructive. Charles Pathé and Leon Gaumont of France began building huge film empires in 1896. Charles and his three brothers formed Pathé Frères, bent on controlling all branches of the French film industry through manufacturing equipment, production and distribution of films, and ownership of theaters. Artistic innovation by the school of Brighton in England and the development of trick photography by individuals such as Frenchman Georges Méliès, were changing the very nature of motion pictures.

In the United States, Edison faced major competition from American Mutoscope and Biograph Company and Vitagraph Company. While the history of Vitagraph was less spectacular than Biograph, it stayed in the market longer. The founder, J. Stuart Blackton, an Englishman who had been a reporter and a cartoonist for the *New York World*, first acquired a Vitascope franchise, then copied the machine and made pictures of his own. He used a name for his company as close to Vitascope as he could legally do so.

While the competition in the burgeoning motion picture industry became increasingly ruthless, the new companies were responding to the public appetite for higher-quality projected images and more and better films. The peepshow machines were a passing curiosity. And initially, the large-screen motion pictures earned a less-than-exalted reputation as "chasers" in vaudeville theaters, since they were normally the concluding act that signalled the end of the performance. However, vaudeville theaters were an obvious place to introduce large-screen motion pictures, and the films were quite popular with the audiences. Edison premiered the Vitascope at Koster and Bial's music hall on April 23, 1896, and rival companies sought out their own vaudeville houses.

Movies themselves quickly matured from set vaudeville skits, nature scenes, and demonstrations to films with a story line, such as Méliès's *The Damnation of Faust* (1898) and Edwin S. Porter's *The Great Train Robbery* (1903). The latter, filmed in New Jersey, was a one-reeler that told a complete story in fourteen scenes with no titles. Violence, humor, and special effects carried the action and made Porter the leading film maker of his day.

A new mass medium was being born, following in the wake of the daily newspaper, the telegraph, and the telephone. More available leisure time, increase in literacy, and broader publicity for sports and various recreational activities in the late nineteenth century enhanced the growth of motion pictures.

In its early years, especially, motion pictures were an urban phenomenon. The audiences came from patrons of live theater or vaudeville, from middle-class people who had never attended theaters because of religious beliefs, and from the large urban working class, who had access to very few other forms of recreation. While the industrial cities provided employment opportunities, amenities such as public playgrounds and other inexpensive forms of entertainment were not widely available to those on the lower end of the class system. The movies, as well as the amusement parks (such as Coney Island) and spectator sports (especially baseball), had a vast impact on the urban quality of life at the turn of the century.

The emergence of a broad market for motion pictures fueled the flames of competition. With each passing year the stakes were greater. But the competition was destructive for many companies in the late 1890s because neither professional conduct nor the protection of law curbed the excesses of manufacturers of equipment, producers of films, and exhibitors.

After receiving his original camera patent in August 31, 1897, Edison authorized a series of infringement suits to drive competitors out of the market. He bypassed Raff and Gammon by going into direct sales. And he fought to reduce the influence of film producers, distributors, and exhibitors through harassment and by making his case in the press, in trade journals, and through circulars. Edison even claimed that he owned the rights to all loops because of Armat's patent on the Latham loop, incorporated into the Vitascope.

But even Armat took to the courts, dissatisfied with Edison for taking full credit for the Vitascope. Seeking a way around this dilemma, Edison began manufacturing his own projection machine—the Projecting Kinetoscope—in 1897, only two years after marketing Armat's device. Cheaper and easier to operate, it marked a major commitment to the new motion picture business. Armat in turn sued everyone who used his loop projector. Edison succeeded against the Lumières, American Mutoscope and Biograph, and Vitagraph because the courts initially upheld Edison's patent. However, the victories were short-lived when the courts reversed the claim.

It was becoming apparent that the patent battles were destructive to the fledgling industry. There were approximately five hundred legal actions, with two hundred making their way to the courts. Thomas Armat exhorted the Edison forces to consider some form of cooperation. He wrote to Gilmore in April 1903, "One of the unfortunate facts in this business is that it requires but little capital to go into it and it attracts a class of people who have much of the fakir or cheap showman in his makeup and the business will sink to his level if thrown open to him."

Beginning in 1909 and lasting until 1915, the Motion Picture Patents Company (MPPC) reversed the trend of cutthroat competition and brought a degree of order to the industry. A licensing system provided the model for the MPPC, which got its impetus from Edison's competitors, worn down by the patent battles and facing financial ruin. Companies including Armat Moving Picture Company, Essanay, Kalem Company, Selig, Vitagraph, and Pathé Frères realized that they could not escape Edison's camera patents through invention and recommended a "royalty proposition" that would be beneficial to all. From the vantage point of the Edison Manufacturing Company, the arrangement was attractive if Biograph, its chief rival in the industry, was left out and ultimately eliminated and if the arrangement succeeded in keeping out new competitors.

While focusing on the issue of licensing manufacturers, other key aspects of the industry were not confronted. For example, despite Edison Company guidelines, many film distributors and exhibitors continued to deal in damaged or pirated films. While quick profits were made, the quality of the films shown diminished—not to mention the skimming in producers' profits through the use of bootlegged film.

The increased intensity of the battle between Edison and Biograph brought the warring parties together in 1908. In an attempt to stop Edison from pushing independents out of the market, Biograph had purchased the patent to the Latham loop and served injunctions on manufacturers affiliated with Edison. The decision of the circuit court to uphold the patent led to a real attempt at compromise in the summer of 1908.

"A Plan to Reorganize the Motion Picture Business in the United States" became the structure for the MPPC. The formal signing of the trust agreement took place at a lavish banquet held in Edison's library at the West Orange laboratory. The agreement merged Biograph and Edison interests, along with Vitagraph, Essanay, Lubin, Selig, Kalem, Méliès, and Pathé. MPPC agreed to share legal rights to machine patents and to keep competitors out of the business. Members also agreed not to sell or lease to any distributor who bought a film from any other company. It also established an exclusive contract with Eastman Kodak Company for commercial quality 35mm raw film stock. Licensed film exchanges combined to make the General Film Company, who rented films only to exhibitors who paid a weekly licensing fee and agreed to show MPPC films exclusively.

The MPPC generally fit the pattern of trust development in the early twentieth century in such industries as petroleum, sugar, and whiskey. The model for MPPC closely resembled the business combine in the field of electronics, in which General Electric merged with several small firms in order to control patents and to curb competition. In this sense, the MPPC was hardly novel; it was an example of the most up-to-date business practices of the day.

Of course, no anti-monopolist looked upon the MPPC as a paragon of virtue or an expression of an idealized competitive market. However, the MPPC had a major impact on rationalizing the practices in and expanding the markets of the American film industry. Better production scheduling and an emphasis on quality allowed American filmmakers to wrest control of the market from foreign domination. A policy of renovation and an effort to acquire fire and accident insurance improved the theaters. The move to end the outright sale of films and the development of an elaborate rental system ended the use of damaged and old prints.

Turmoil in the industry did not end so easily. "Trust wars" replaced "patent wars" as independents tried to grab the domestic market from MPPC. In its turn, MPPC sought to invade the international market. And as in other industries of the era, opponents used government anti-trust legislation to restore competition. When MPPC cancelled William Fox's New York Film Rental Company distribution exchange, a restraint of trade lawsuit under the Sherman Antitrust Act led to a judgment against MPPC on October 1, 1915, sustained in a higher court in 1918.

In a broader sense, MPPC's own restrictive practices were almost impossible to enforce, and independents ate away at the market. Other problems, such as the end of the exclusive contract with Eastman and the loss of revenue in Europe due to World War I, aided in crippling the once powerful trust.

Edison had been a rather late player in the battle for the film projection market. Yet once the tangible rewards were staked out, he entered with a vengeance. By 1912 the motion picture department was the most profitable part of the West Orange enterprise, with Edison receiving a major share of the income from MPPC between 1909 and 1914. But this was short-lived prosperity. Escalating competition and falling prices forced him out of the market, and in 1918 the motion picture business was sold to Lincold and Parker Film Company.

As in the case of the phonograph, Edison proved to be adept in envisioning other uses for motion pictures. He foresaw educational, home, and business uses as alternatives or complements to mass entertainment. On more than one occasion he stated that the educational use of the motion picture was to be a prime function. He rather boldly told a reporter in 1922 that one of the great missions of the motion picture was "to educate, elevate, and inspire." "I believe," he added, "that the motion picture is destined to revolutionize our educational system, and that in a few years it will supplant largely, if not entirely, the use of textbooks in our schools." He marketed a Home Kinetoscope for bringing motion pictures into the home and for providing educational opportunities away from school. He became involved in producing educational and industrial films. And he continued to labor over a device that merged film and phonograph. The end product was the Kinetophone, a precursor to the "talkies."

The momentum of his previous successes, his exalted place in the world of invention and business, his confidence in his abilities, and his opportunism had ultimately made the motion picture business irresistible to Thomas Edison. His involvement in the industry was hardly his finest accomplishment, bringing to the surface his worst impulses as a businessman.

Time was changing Edison. No longer the boy from the Midwest, nor a struggling telegrapher and inventor, nor manager of a small laboratory of close-knit workers, he was a major industrialist with little time to sneak a cat nap or mull over a nagging problem. Bound by his commitments and his celebrity, he was now the establishment, less frequently the trend setter.

CHAPTER NINE

The Corporate Image

❖
❖

A suit to dissolve the Standard Oil Trust was filed in 1907, with hearings beginning in September. Special Prosecutor Frank Kellogg and his staff took testimony from approximately four hundred people in the ensuing fifteen months. In May 1911 the United States Supreme Court decreed that Standard Oil Company had to divest itself of all subsidiaries. In a twenty-thousand-word opinion, Chief Justice Edward D. White stated that the "very genius for commercial development and organization" that created the trust had led it to form a monopoly, driving others from the field and excluding them from their "right to trade."

The establishment of the modern petroleum industry commenced with the formation of John D. Rockefeller's Standard Oil Company. Rockefeller began his career in produce merchandizing in Cleveland but turned to oil in the 1860s. Standard's ability to dominate the early oil business was extraordinary. It quickly became an integrated firm with control of its oil from well head to market.

Company officials soon realized that Standard's continued growth demanded a new, more sophisticated organizational structure. Samuel T.C. Dodd, Standard's astute counsel, recommended the development of a "trust"—an old device but in a new setting. Through reorganization, nine trustees would hold the certificates of Standard's companies "in trust." In 1882 the Standard Oil Trust was formed, providing the firm with tax advantages and more flexibility in controlling pricing and other features of the oil industry. The Ohio courts nullified the agreement in 1892, but the Cleveland-based company reorganized in New Jersey where the laws were more congenial. By 1904 Standard once again controlled about ninety percent of the country's kerosene production (the major petroleum product at the time).

Muckrakers and other critics of big business made careers out of battling the oil giant. Ida Tarbell, in her *History of the Standard Oil Company* (1904), commented that the combine "has always been rich in youth as well as greed, in brains as well as unscrupulousness." In an 1881 issue of *Atlantic Monthly*, sharp-edged reformer Henry Demarest Lloyd observed that "America has the proud satisfaction of having furnished the world with the greatest, wisest, and meanest monopoly known to history."

The protest against Standard came from many beyond the muckraking press, especially small independents and other competitors who found themselves caught in its grasp. However, to their dismay, the dissolution did not wreck Standard Oil. Competition from new giants—Gulf, the Texas Company (Texaco), and Shell—and a burgeoning market in fuel oil and gasoline transformed the industry from a monopoly to an oligopoly, pushing Standard from absolute dominance to shared control.

Standard, nonetheless, had left an indelible mark on big business. Dodd's corporate model led to larger companies that undermined the competitive market but also inspired more efficient organization. The startling success of the Standard Oil Trust encouraged other firms to seek monopolies in their own industries such as sugar, tobacco, steel, and whiskey. At the same time, the 1911 dissolution helped to prolong the antitrust movement and paved the way for cases against similar combines.

The rise and fall of Thomas Edison's movie trust clearly followed the business trends begun by the Standard. But Edison's far-flung interests, while mirroring other business ventures in scale and breadth, did not match the growing list of integrated companies in structure and organization. That was to change. In the wake of the 1911 dissolution, Thomas A. Edison, Inc., was formed.

Business enterprise had undergone other major changes in the nineteenth and early twentieth centuries. In many industries, the traditional American firm—small, personally owned and managed—lost ground to the modern corporation—large, well financed, professionally managed. In the 1840s railroad and telegraph companies established new patterns of administrative structure while stimulating a revolution in transportation, communications, and the production and distribution of goods. The technological innovation that provided the large-scale manufacturing capability also stimulated the development of new managerial techniques. The mass-production system built on these technical and organizational changes, along with mass marketing created a truly national economy by the turn of the century. Integrated firms with salaried managers and centralized administrative structures (pioneered by Standard Oil) acquired a powerful advantage in the marketplace. By the 1880s some companies chose the merger as a route to bigness; by 1900 many businesses became multinational enterprises.

For the most part, these major trends had eluded the numerous Edison companies in their early years. While the Wizard tried to remain in personal control of his myriad activities, contemporary economy and the shifting fortunes of his ventures worked against him. In addition, the seduction of the laboratory and the impulse for invention grew stronger in Edison as the onerous duties of running the businesses grew more tedious.

The reorganization of Edison's companies into a consolidated Thomas A. Edison, Inc., moved the operations into alignment with modern business practices. To some extent, it freed Edison from much of the daily routine that took him away from the lab, and was ruining his health.

Those involved in the restructuring realized that while drastic internal changes were necessary, the public focus had to remain on Edison. A memorandum to the heads of all departments issued on March 1, 1911, noted that "Beginning March 2nd, all correspondence, orders and other matter relating to the National Phonograph Company and the Edison Business Phonograph Company must be signed in the name of 'Thomas A. Edison, Incorporated.' This especially applies to our relations with outside people." Another letter stated that the principal reason for the new company epithet was to perpetuate the name of Edison and to "bring home more firmly to the public the fact that this is Mr. Edison's personal business and that his personality stands behind it." The new name had great advertising value ". . . because the word 'Incorporated' can be omitted or printed in very small type in advertisements, so that the advertisements will make a strong personal plea." Ironically, personalizing the name of the corporation was in stark contrast with the new managerial style.

Converging circumstances had led to the decision to incorporate and consolidate several businesses. In the past, Edison simply set up a new company and a new manufacturing facility whenever he developed a new product. As a result, there was little overall planning and little or no coordination among the various units. Despite the flurry of activity in the new motion picture business and the central role of Edison in the MPPC, the real heart of his enterprise was the phonograph. But the cylinder business had peaked in 1907, stymied by a depression in that year and increased competition from foreign manufacturers and the introduction of the disc phonograph. Within the National Phonograph Company problems arose because of key court defeats at the hands of franchisees and because of failed experiments with new inventions. Business woes were exacerbated by a disappointing showing in the motion picture operations and potent competition in the cement business. The risky undertaking in the storage battery field also was draining capital. Profits from successful companies and Edison's own money (at a rate of one hundred thousand dollars a month) were being dumped into the venture to keep it afloat.

In addition to the quavering business activity was the matter of Edison's health. In 1900 and 1901 he became seriously ill. A few years later he had to undergo emergency surgery for an ear infection, which impaired his hearing even more than before. Only in his fifties, Edison was faltering. In 1907 he went so far as to announce that he was going to retire from business. While this proved an impulsive reaction, years of intense activity were taking their toll. Even the mention of retirement necessitated some action by key staff members and financial supporters to protect the conglomerate of companies and to insure that they were organized in such a way as to continue without the inventor's guiding hand.

As a stop-gap measure, company executives tried to wean Edison from some of the daily routine of the various enterprises. Keep the operations moving along smoothly while Edison tinkered in the laboratory—that seemed to be the prevailing wisdom. But such a simple plan was difficult to implement. The companies were diverse, with operations scattered throughout New York and New Jersey, and the legal and financial relationship among the units was mind-boggling.

Company executives pleaded with Edison to cut back on unprofitable ventures—especially the cement company—at least until new products could replenish earnings. Frank L. Dyer, who had replaced William Gilmore as the president of the National Phonograph Company in 1908, realized that the Edison empire could not lumber along in such dinosaur fashion. He pressed for a centralized organization. A lawyer like the Standard's mastermind Samuel Dodd, Dyer had served as Edison's chief patent counsel in 1897. Under his direction, the National Phonograph Company (NPC) became the core around which Thomas A. Edison, Inc., was established in 1911.

Thomas A. Edison, Inc., was capitalized at about twelve million dollars. Departments were set up for specific products, and a management system mirrored most large corporations at the time. Dyer served as chief executive officer and general manager with layers of vice presidents and middle managers below him. Edison was the president and sat on an executive committee with Dyer and two vice presidents. Under the provisions of the company charter he would "dictate policies of the company" and had a broad veto power over the action of subordinate officers and department heads.

A press release stated that changing the name of the company to Thomas A. Edison, Incorporated "is the first step of a movement to combine under one head all the companies now engaged here in the manufacture and sale of Edison phonographs and motion pictures." On March 3, the *Rochester Herald* ran the startling headline, "Wife Controls Edison Combine." The accompanying story, however, went on to state in less dramatic fashion that "Mr. Edison does not figure as a stockholder in the new company, Mrs. Edison holding the control."

Besides centralized management, the new company propped up weaker companies with the earnings of the stronger ones. The New Jersey Patents Company, the Edison Manufacturing Company, the Business Phonograph Company, and NPC were absorbed into Thomas A. Edison, Inc. Less profitable companies were temporarily excluded, while some companies kept their names but were managed by the corporation. In particular, the business phonograph—or dictating machine—benefited most from the infusion of capital into marketable products. For the first time resources necessary to continue research and development and effectively to promote the device became available.

By 1915 TAE, Inc., matured from a diversified business into a multidivisional enterprise with divisions for the various products controlled by a central administration. Under the new system, costing became the prime interest of upper management, with accountants gaining substantially more influence in a business once dominated by an inventor/entrepreneur. In most cases, professional managers at the divisional levels focused on running the individual companies, while engineers and other specialists concentrated on design and testing.

The reorganization even affected the research center. In the more competitive markets of the twentieth century, the goal was to have the laboratory provide engineering support for the manufacturing units. While Edison had a decision-making role in the company, the experimental techniques that he perfected at Menlo Park and West Orange did not suit the financial goals of the corporation. The West Orange facility ceased to be the heart of the enterprise and was no longer the only Edison facility involved in research and development. In the 1890s another lab was established at Silver Lake, which set a precedent for the building of similar satellite facilities. A movie studio was established in the Bronx in 1905; a recording studio was placed on Fifth Avenue in New York in 1906. Many of the factories set up their own testing laboratories. The trend toward concentrating research and development, emblematic of Menlo Park, was moving toward decentralization and specialization in the early twentieth century.

Edison continued to relish laboratory work, which kept him in close contact with the chief engineer. He was especially close to Miller Reese Hutchison, who replaced George Bliss in that post in 1912. The relationship between Edison and Hutchison defined the activities of the laboratory and strongly influenced the Edison enterprises in other ways. Born into a landed Alabama family, Hutchison eschewed the patrician life to become an inventor/entrepreneur. He received his first patent at the age of eighteen and produced a hearing aid called the Acousticon. Mina, in fact, bought one for her husband, which he wore on special occasions. Hutchison also developed an electric Klaxon horn and a self-starter for automobiles, and even attempted to develop a storage battery of his own.

A frequent caller to the Edison laboratory, Hutchison had impressed the Wizard in 1910 when he brought several navy officers for a visit that netted a large order for batteries. At that point Edison agreed to pay Hutchison a regular commission on the sale of batteries. The two men grew even closer as Hutchison continued to march all the important men he knew through West Orange. In April 1911 Edison asked Hutchison to move his office into the laboratory, offering him space and experiment facilities.

For a time, Hutchison became one of Edison's closest confidants. He took up the role of a second-in-command held by friend and co-inventor Charles Batchelor before his death in 1910. Hutchison appealed to Edison as "one of the boys," with a high energy level and an enthusiasm for developing new products. Edison and his protégé stimulated a great deal of activity, leading to the production of models for new Kinetoscopes, disc phonographs, and dictating machines. Hutchison, for his part, brought order to the research center, rearranging the third floor, inspecting machinery, and even installing a time clock. (The Old Man was issued card number 1.) Edison, however, drew the line on the efficiency move when it came to personnel, refusing to authorize the dismissal of any devoted employee no matter how unproductive. While he bristled at labor unions and paid meager wages, he continued to prize loyalty and hard work above all else.

Hutchison, an opportunist with dreams of his own, had some key business interests closely linked to the products being developed at West Orange, especially the storage battery. After revamping the laboratory, he devoted an inordinate amount of time to acquiring sales commissions, often turning over routine engineering work to his assistants. Hutchison was making the most of his relationship with the boss, but he also was making strong enemies among the other leaders of TAE, Inc., especially Charles Edison and Stephen B. Mambert.

Charles Edison, who graduated from MIT, joined the enterprise in 1913. He had aspirations—which his mother supported—to take over the business after his father's death. Mambert, an efficiency engineer who joined the company as financial executive in 1914 and who wielded the principal power at the time, told Edison that Hutchison "was entirely insincere in his oft-repeated show of affection for the company." His business dealings seemed to sustain that view. Representatives of the federal government, especially, recoiled at having to pay a middleman's commission to Hutchison instead of dealing directly with those in charge at TAE, Inc. The enmity of Charles Edison and Mambert, and Hutchison's own financial maneuvering, eventually forced him out.

The reorganization of Edison's companies was a case of facing the inevitable or being left behind in the shuffle. Edison's patents were the bedrock of his enterprises, but without the proper organization his products could never meet competition in the marketplace. And on the heels of establishing TAE, Inc., Edison was mindful of the rigors of competition. "We have been going on the theory of compelling people to compete," he stated in a December 1911 interview. "Competition results in the destruction of the weaker of the country by the stronger, and under this system, if continued, the time will come when a few individuals or great concerns will control the country. Competition of this kind is war. It means death to the weaker. Cooperation means life . . ."

The Sherman Antitrust Act (1890), the first national attempt to confront the problem of monopoly, troubled Edison because it appeared to challenge the legality of contracts made over patent rights. "The men who made the trust law," he argued, "didn't know pig iron from coffins, so far as the producing business is concerned." He had benefited greatly from the legal monopoly over the manufacture, use, and sale of his inventions for seventeen years afforded under patent law. But he also was concerned that the antimonopoly effort would curb industrial consolidation and thus promote cutthroat competition that would not only hurt the weaker companies but work against efficient business operation. Excessive competition led to price cutting and ultimately selling below cost in order to capture a larger portion of the market. This in turn resulted in the production of lower-quality merchandise to offset short-term losses. Price stability was very important. Money could be made on volume sales, not through the precariousness of price wars. "Make it against the law," he said, "to combine to increase prices, not for the corporation, but for the responsible officers of the corporation."

As early as 1891 he had recommended enforcement of price guidelines through trade associations. Business cooperation was preferable to cutthroat competition on the one hand and governmental regulation on the other. His views mirrored those of many corporate leaders who sought stability in the market as the proper environment for growth and development, especially through industry-wide associations. Edison, however, did not have a fully developed theory. Instead, he responded to those issues that seemed most immediately threatening to his business interests.

On trusts he was ambivalent and inconsistent. In an 1891 notebook he stated flatly that "There's no such thing possible as a good trust." In 1909 he helped to establish the MPPC, which may have seemed to fit the spirit of cooperation, but looked suspiciously like a trust. In 1912 he fell in line behind the Bull Moose insurgency of Theodore Roosevelt, seemingly buying into Roosevelt's business views by stating that "Trusts are good things, but ought to be regulated the same as railroads are regulated." And in words clearly reminiscent of the progressive spirit of the day, he asserted on much broader terms that "Our production, our factory laws, our charities, our relations between capital and labor, our distribution—all wrong, out of gear. We've stumbled along for a while trying to run a new civilization in old ways, and we've got to start to make this world over." In an aside, which reflected a clear self-appraisal of his own career, he added, "Building a new world out of old material, that's what some of us have been doing all our lives."

Insofar as his views extended from his own actions to a larger model, Edison was often inconsistent but not intentionally deceptive. He believed firmly that the United States was the perfect place to pursue his goals without the fetters imposed by other political or economic systems. Nationalism incorporated what he perceived to be the advantages of a capitalist system if not a completely open market economy. In the late nineteenth and early twentieth centuries, especially, he stood foursquare with his fellow big businessmen in his view of the limits of the competitive market.

His enthusiasm for Teddy Roosevelt and political reform came from his belief that progressivism was "a young man's movement." "There are a lot of people who die in the head after they are fifty," he said. "They're the ones who get shocked if you propose anything that wasn't going on when they were boys. It's the way the world goes—the young push ahead and do things, and the old stand back. I hope I'll always be with the young."

Edison had never before been so malleable in his working life—he resisted AC power, the disc phonograph, and the internal combustion engine. But he never gave up wanting to build "a new world out of old material" and sometimes could be persuaded to change outdated methods in pursuit of his goals. To Edison, developing inventions and products of enduring utility contributed to the material progress of the world. His determination to make a profit, while simultaneously improving the quality of life, was guided by his voracious need to be part of the inventive moment. It remained to be seen if Edison could adapt to the new goals set for his businesses under the 1911 consolidation.

As the role of West Orange changed, so did the function of Edison's businesses. Maintaining a respectable share of the market became more important than developing astounding new inventions. Improving the phonograph and motion picture progress received the greatest attention in the 1910s.

The development of the storage battery, which consumed much of Edison's own time until World War I, was a throwback of sorts to the glory days of unbridled inquiry and research. For many years at West Orange the search for a practical storage battery had consumed resources rather than producing profits. It was not so graciously identified by some, along with ore milling and cement production, as the latest Edison folly.

But Edison's dogged commitment was not simply an exercise in chasing windmills. To produce such a technology would be to revolutionize the use of electricity, that is, to liberate it from the power plant and the cord. The uses for such a device were abundant, as Edison himself realized. In October 1911 he jotted down sixty "uses for the Edison Battery" including motive power (for streetcars and locomotives, taxicabs and trucks, submarines and lawnmowers), lighting (inspectors' lights and lanterns, lighting for isolated houses, running lights for boats), household uses (doorbells, burglar alarms, player pianos), and numerous other applications (storing solar, tidal, and wave power; starters for automobiles; power for windmills).

That Edison's ultimate success was limited, and the research and development a major drag on the resources of his other enterprises, does not detract from the significance of the work. The storage battery was one of but a few research projects that was not a refinement of an earlier invention but a leap into a relatively new field, which allowed Edison to recapture some of the intensity of his earlier career and to take time away from life as an industrial magnate.

Edison's vision for the use of the battery also brought him back to his urban market. In attempting to develop an electric car that could compete on equal terms with the internal combustion engine, he directed his energies to the unique transportation needs of the city. Eventually, the electric car lost out to the popularity of the Model T, which came to dominate both the urban and rural transportation markets in the United States. But the work with electric vehicles carved out a niche in the market that held out possibilities for the future.

The work on the storage battery continued to demonstrate the promoter—or huckster—in Edison. Once again he took an invention with enormous potential and convinced people that success was just around the corner. At the very least, the publicity surrounding the storage battery kept Edison in the public eye, if not as the driving force in the boardroom of TAE, Inc.

The storage battery itself was a rather old device, originating with the Voltaic pile in 1800 or to Frenchman Gaston Plante's work on "secondary currents" and "polarization voltages" in 1859. All electric cells—two or more cells in combination comprise a battery—include a container, a solution of some sort, and plates. The solution can be a liquid or paste electrolyte—that is, a conductor that undergoes chemical change when an electric current passes through it. The plates act as electrodes that collect positively and negatively charged particles from the solution. In a storage battery, electrical energy is stored as chemical energy which is then converted into electrical current. A storage—or secondary—battery is recharged by running a current through it, unlike a primary battery that is recharged by replacement of spent parts.

The early work led to the study of saline solutions as electrolytes. The most important early invention was the pasted plate process of Camille Faure in 1881, which led to the practice of pasting lead salts to plates. Other research and invention slowly added to the knowledge required to produce a battery of increased wattage and reduced weight for various practical uses. The Europeans—not Americans—were in the forefront of the development. By the 1850s C.W. Siemens and others synthesized earlier experiments and produced the first lead-acid storage battery.

Between 1850 and 1880 several inventors from Europe and the United States attempted to apply the lead-acid battery to long-distance telegraphy and for use in arc lighting. While the efforts did not prove to be commercially successful, they revealed a range of possible functions for storage batteries.

Before the commercialization of arc lighting at the end of the 1870s, all electric current came from primary batteries. And since primary batteries generate and store energy, there was little room for the storage battery. Dynamos separated generation from the storage of electricity, and the storage battery acquired a potential market in the area of electromagnetic generation of electrical power. Yet the most obvious application was for motive power, especially streetcars, where self-propulsion would be a distinct advantage over expensive and dangerous third rails or overhead conductors. Efforts to produce a commercially successful system proved futile, however.

Another potential use was a power for isolated lighting systems, especially since central-station power was only applicable in densely populated urban areas in the nascent days of that technology. However, the batteries available were bulky, difficult to maintain, and produced noxious vapors. A large bank of them in the cellar of a house could be unwieldy as well as dangerous.

More practical was to integrate storage batteries into the operation of the central station or substations. The batteries could keep labor costs down by "load levelling." For example, generating equipment could be run at peak level during one shift, producing enough power to meet customer demand and at the same time charging the batteries. During the remainder of the day, when demand for electricity dropped, current could be produced by the batteries alone. This worked especially well in the last two decades of the nineteenth century when demand for electrical power was still relatively low. As a result, batteries used for load levelling—and also as a backup energy source—proved to be the bulk of business for the fledgling companies at that time.

The battery industry was by no means thriving in the 1880s and 1890s. The deluge of patent applications—six hundred between 1881 and 1895 in the United States alone—indicated a strong interest. But well into the new century, the industry suffered many stops and starts. Through the late 1880s, failure of many installations linked to lighting systems drew skepticism as well as the reluctance of American electrical engineers to embrace the new technology. Even with the appearance of high-quality batteries, the case was yet to be made.

Until the mid-1890s the American storage battery industry only drifted as Europeans continued to make headway with new designs. Several breakthroughs led to a growing American leadership in the field by the early twentieth century. Large central stations began to install what were agreed to be more dependable batteries; even several Edison stations in major cities began to install them. Most significantly, major segments of the electric streetcar industry began to use the batteries in their powerhouses for load-levelling purposes. The development of more portable versions extended their use to a wide array of other fields. Charles Kettering's invention of the electric starter in 1911 revolutionized the automobile industry and opened a major new market for storage batteries.

Edison had shown some interest during the early developmental stage in the 1880s. The need to find a power source for the phonograph led to experiments with primary and secondary batteries. In 1889 Edison established the Primary Battery Division which produced copper-oxide batteries under an agreement with Felix Lalande. Railroads proved to be the major customer for the Edison-Lalande primary cell. However, in establishing his DC lighting and power-generation systems, Edison had more faith in using additional generators for load levelling than adding the available lead-acid batteries. Whether he questioned the reliability of this product or was unwilling to tamper with the power-generation system he had just completed is uncertain. But it is clear that he had little interest in entering the field in a major way at the time.

By 1899, however, Edison set out to design a new type using an alkaline solution as the electrolyte, which would not corrode the metal. Not surprisingly, his quest coincided with the newly found commercial viability of the lead-acid batteries and recent research on alkaline storage batteries.

The initial research took Edison and his staff of almost ninety chemists, physicists, and technicians five years to complete. Ultimately, they conducted more than ten thousand experiments. Edison was convinced that the bulky lead-acid battery had to be replaced with a lighter, more durable one that would have broad application, particularly in the transportation field.

His first efforts to find an appropriate electrolyte in 1899 led him to several different cells. The results were inconclusive after a year of research, and he generated only one patent for a zinc-mercury type. He soon gravitated toward the zinc-copper cell because the active materials were relatively cheap and would give him more of a competitive edge with the established lead-acid cell. In addition, most of the prior experiments focused on the zinc and copper combination.

Edison continued his search, turning next to cadmium-copper. But he gave up on that combination in 1900 because no inexpensive source of cadmium could be found. In late December he conducted his first experiments with nickel and iron, and by March 1901 he had applied for patents on nickel-iron and cobalt-iron batteries. In April he built a new chemical plant at Silver Lake, New Jersey, initially to carry out experiments with nickel and iron, which proved to be the combination he was looking for.

By 1903 he had decided to use the combination of nickel and iron with a potassium hydroxide electrolyte. He manufactured this battery as the Type E, which sold well in 1903 and 1904. However, leakage and rapid drop in electrical capacity after brief use suggested that the battery required further testing. He recalled all of the defective cells in November 1904—at his own expense—despite the admonition of his financial advisers. In 1909 he introduced a new nickel flake cell—Type A—which proved to be a substantial improvement over Type E.

Unlike his work on the filament and other trial-and-error processes, Edison's work on the storage battery was more systematic, more dependent on careful literature and patent searches and on the investigation of promising earlier experiments. When it came to testing a new battery his old trial-and-error instincts crept back. As he stated in a 1908 letter to a friend, "This method of developing an automobile by loading it up to the limit & running it maximum speed over the worst road you can find will teach in 2 months more than can be learned in 10 years in the usual way & is highly commercial. Any vehicle that can be made to stand one month will be a big comcl [*sic*] success."

The process of marketing a commercially viable storage battery proved very difficult. The Wizard supported much of the Edison Storage Battery Company with money out of his own pocket. By 1910 the company's indebtedness was $1.3 million, which was more than the capital stock of the company. In all, Edison spent $1.9 million in the development and manufacture of the battery. Despite the financial risks, Edison was bent on developing battery power for transportation. He sensed a marketing opportunity that he was unwilling to pass up. "In fifteen years," Edison predicted in August 1910, "more electricity will be sold for electric vehicles than for light." A few years earlier he had bragged that his battery would so reduce the price of automobiles that "It will settle the horse!" He did not like horses anyway, much preferring "a motor with a governor on it," and predicted that the urban horse would become "a luxury, a toy, and a pet."

The hype was unrelenting during the developmental phase of the storage battery. It was typical for Edison to entice the public with advanced announcements of a marvelous new invention, whetting their appetite and priming them for what was to come. He would revolutionize surface vehicles by means of a perfected storage battery, he bragged. Automobiles would be priced within the reach of most Americans, he promised. He told a gathering of the National Electric Light Association that he had invented a battery that could fit into a suitcase "and it can run a car, truck, automobile, or vehicle of any kind until the power is used up, and then recharged in less than three minutes, ready for service as before." Prematurely, he boasted to reporters, "At last I have solved the problem of decent existence for the poor man—and to the rich, too, I can hold out a glad message. The dangerless electric auto, going a hundred miles without recharge, at twenty miles per hour, if you like, is an accomplished fact."

Whether uncontrolled exuberance about his new venture or a deliberate strategy to increase sales, his claims were cheered by those who came to expect a minor miracle from him regularly. But over the years Edison's dramatic proclamations about other inventions had begun to attract skeptics, and with good reason. In a November 1907 issue of the British journal *Autocar,* an unidentified electrical engineer chided Edison for claiming more praise for his laboratory work on the storage battery than it deserved. "For practical purposes," he argued, Edison's alkaline battery was no better than the older lead-acid battery. "We appeal in the strongest terms that we know of to Mr. Edison to consult his own dignity, and the dignity of the profession he represents, *and to cease giving childish statements to the world.*"

Yet Edison's interest in developing an electrical power source to run vehicles was more than a marketing pose; it grew out of a genuine fascination with automobiles and their potential, especially in cities. "The ever-present problem with New York is traffic," he stated in one interview. "Its ever-increasing population and the way to enable New Yorkers to get to and from their homes and still live within the confines of the city make this traffic question one of continual importance."

He was, to be sure, an automobile buff who relished outings and was exhilarated by a wild high-speed ride in the country. He also was fascinated by the delicious problem of adapting an inexpensive, clean, convenient, self-contained source of power to a motorized vehicle. In a 1910 letter to Samuel Insull, Edison could hardly contain his enthusiasm about the application of the storage battery to the automobile: "It seems too bad that all of the electrical people must go through the long dreary educational process like we did with the light, and other things—But they will, in time understand, that the greatest market for electricity will be the electric vehicle because now they have the only missing link—to wit a reliable, low depreciation storage of power device, . . ."

However, Edison embraced the electric automobile at the moment when the internal combustion engine was asserting primacy, and well before he was able to perfect the storage battery. By 1908, when Henry Ford put his mass-produced Model T on the market, the motor car ceased to be a toy for the rich. Cheap fuel and the higher speeds and greater cruising distance gave them a clear edge over the electrics. In addition, Kettering's development of the electric starter for gasoline automobiles made it possible for anyone to operate the motorcar without a hand crank.

Edison's work on the electric car was not wasted. The numerous reliability tests and experiments with various types of batteries led to the development of a storage battery suited to motive power by 1910. While success did not come in the glamorous field of automobile manufacturing, Edison had good success with electric trucks and other applications suited to the cities. The electric delivery truck could make rounds during the day and return to the garage at night for a charge. The continual stopping and starting during a delivery run were much less of a burden for electrics than for gasoline-powered vehicles. Batteries were adapted to streetcars as well, but with less success. Motorcars equipped with self-starters eventually cut into the electric truck business and the potential for the urban vehicle, which did not suffer the pollution problems of the internal combustion engine, was never truly realized.

The refined Edison storage batteries, however, came to be known for long life and dependability, making them well suited for stand-by uses in power plants, railway signaling, train lights, and miners' lamps, and for an array of military uses. Out of a spoiled vision in transportation, a wide field of uses emerged and began returning profits to Edison on his heavy investment.

As World War I approached, Edison himself and his business ventures had reached maturity. The torrid inventive activity of the past had slowed sufficiently to provide time for reevaluation and planning. If Edison no longer wielded all the power in his business empire, or was not hell-bent to be at the heart of every decision, he now had the luxury of choosing how to spend his time. A secure man, emotionally and financially, he was losing the compulsion to outdo himself or to prove himself to the world. It was time to begin savoring his accomplishments and celebrity.

CHAPTER TEN

The Wizard at War

On January 7, 1914, an old French crane boat, *Alexandre La Valley,* made the first complete passage through the Pacific locks of the Panama Canal. Army engineer George W. Goethals and his crew had accomplished what others had only dreamed about and speculated about for generations—a waterway equal to a channel, as one writer noted, "dug ten feet deep and fifty-five feet wide from Maine to Oregon." The completed engineering marvel allowed ships to pass through six huge locks that would raise the vessels approximately eight-five feet above sea level at the Continental Divide and then lower them at the other end of the Isthmus. The horizontal/vertical journey shortened by almost eight thousand miles a trip between New York and San Francisco at one-tenth the cost of transit around the tip of South America.

Plans were made in Washington and San Francisco for colossal opening celebrations scheduled for August, with one hundred warships set to move from Hampton Roads, Virginia, through the canal to San Francisco to attend the opening of the Panama-Pacific International Exposition. But the plans had to be scrapped. The opening was buried on the back pages of the newspapers because it could not compete with the drama, tragedy, and immediacy of thunderheads of war hanging over Europe.

On June 28, 1914, a young Bosnian revolutionary assassinated Archduke Franz Ferdinand, heir to the Austro-Hungarian throne, while on a visit to Sarajevo, the capital of the Austrian province of Bosnia. Serbian nationalists were behind the plot, and one month after the assassination Austria declared war on Serbia. Josef Redlich, a scholar and member of the Reichsrat, summarized the feelings of the times when he wrote in his diary, "Only the sword can save Austria." Accumulated hatreds and suspicion throughout Europe set off a chain of events that quickly spread war across the continent. In time, Asia, Africa, the Middle East, and North America came into the conflict. The United States entered the war in April 1917.

Thomas Edison was pressed into service by his country as war threatened—not as a conscript, of course, but as a spearhead for harnessing science and technology to the preparedness movement and then to the war effort itself. But first a personal tragedy in 1914 jeopardized years of productivity and seemed to tear his world apart. On December 9, 1914, Edison went home for dinner (more customary in his later years) when he received word that fire broke out at the West Orange facility just before 6:00 P.M. Fire companies from eight nearby towns answered the call, but they had to fight the blaze with drastically reduced water pressure due to the extreme cold of winter.

The conflagration started in a shed containing flammable motion picture film stock in the middle of the old Phonograph Works building. It spread rapidly, damaging or destroying thirteen buildings over a four-block area. Astonishingly, the main laboratory escaped harm with irreplaceable moulds and recordings for the phonograph business remaining intact.

On the night of the fire, Edison handed reporters a hastily written statement, "Am pretty well burned out—but tomorrow there will be some rapid mobilizing when I find out where I am at." In a reply to President Woodrow Wilson's telegram of support, he wrote, "Am sure it would please you greatly to watch the people here and to see what American hustling will accomplish in a short period of time." And in another letter he added,

"It's like the old days to have something real to buck up against." In a curious way, the fire brought to Edison's mind victories over other apparently insurmountable struggles.

His son Charles was on hand to help direct the emergency activities, and the Wizard said to him, "Where's Mother? Get her over here, and her friends too, They'll never see a fire like this again." But while he gave several rather upbeat statements to the press, he confided to Charles, "I wonder what we will use for money?" Several of the structures gutted by fire had been built of reinforced concrete, and because of this "fireproof" construction, Edison had insured them at less than one-third their cost. The losses were estimated at one million dollars.

The inventor personally led the clearing of the debris and the rebuilding on the very next day with a crew of fifteen hundred men. Factory space was rented, machinery set up, and new loans negotiated. On January 1, 1915, the company was producing the first disc records as if nothing had happened. The West Orange facility was up and running again.

As a result of the reorganization under Thomas A. Edison, Inc., the decentralization of research and testing activity, and the fire, West Orange became more a manufacturing center than a research facility. It stood at the center of a powerful industry but was now a component rather than the core of the enterprise. Edison himself emerged from the experience with his confidence intact. He may not have been on the brink of a new blockbuster invention, but he entered the latter years of the 1910s as the best example of the American "can-do" philosophy.

With the war raging in Europe, Edison's immediate concern was the effect on his far-flung business empire. After a brief spurt of orders for patriotic films, the overseas motion picture business dwindled. Of even greater significance, the Allied blockade of continental ports cut off his supply of German chemicals essential to the production of storage batteries and phonograph records. Edison required approximately one ton of phenolic resin—used in the manufacture of phonograph records—each day. Rather than seeking alternative supplies, he decided to produce the necessary chemicals himself.

What began as a serious liability turned into an asset, for his Silver Lake plant produced six tons of phenol per day—much of which he could sell to other companies. The venture was so successful that a second phenol plant doubled his capacity. With his own house in order, Edison turned his attention to the national debate over preparedness, that is, whether the United States should prepare for the eventuality of war or simply isolate itself from the conflict. A hint of pacifism entered into his early pronouncements. He told the press that he was "sick at heart" over the war, and that "Making things which kill men is against my fiber." In response to a personal letter he stated that "war is not a biological necessity . . ."

But Edison's political views—though not particularly systematized—pushed him toward preparedness. On August 6, 1914, the day German troops crossed the Belgian border, Edison sent a telegram to the *Chicago Examiner* stating what might be considered his "official" views on the conflict. "Nothing short of the Almighty can stop this war," he wrote. "Civilization is undergoing a surgical operation. It is necessary to settle for all time that Dynastic Militarism shall disappear from the earth. That the people shall rule through constitutional governments. That all races of men may dwell together in amity as they do now in the United States."

His friend Henry Ford, a strong pacifist, was dismayed by Edison's involvement with preparedness. But the Wizard was a staunch patriot. Although he admired German efficiency, French road building and bread making, and the scientific achievement of his peers throughout the continent, he identified more closely with his country than with the international community of scientists. After returning from a vacation in Europe in 1911, he told the press, "I tell you, boys, I felt like kissing the Statue of Liberty when I came up the bay to-day." In a rather backhanded compliment to the English he stated, "Next to Americans the English have the best practical brains." On Paris: "I was disappointed . . . in Paris as the so-called 'City of Light.' It bears no comparison to New York in that respect. The Champs Élysées, which is the most brilliantly illuminated street in the city, looks like twilight compared with Manhattan's 'Great White Way.'" And he concluded, "I am well satisfied, however, to get back to my own country, for I did not see any country on the other side of the ocean that can compare with the United States, if considered as a whole."

Edison well realized the potential for military application of his inventions. Electricity had a range of uses from communications to battery power for submarines and surface vessels. In the mid-1880s he had formed the Edison-Sims Electric Torpedo Company to design and manufacture submarines, torpedoes, and other naval weapons. While the venture came to naught, Edison and Gardiner Sims are credited with designing the first remote-controlled weapon, a torpedo powered by electricity and guided by cables.

His first contract with the navy was during the Spanish-American War. In 1898 Edison suggested that the navy employ a shell containing calcium carbide and calcium phosphide for making enemy ships visible at night. He also convinced them to use some of his motion picture equipment.

Aware of the escalation of war through the development of increasingly sophisticated weapons, Edison had prophesied the use of aerial bombing and high-explosive weapons. Periodically, stories would circulate about the Wizard's "doomsday machine." In France it was rumored in 1892 that Edison was building a super weapon for Germany. All this talk led some writers to make a pulp novel hero of Edison in such classics as "Edison's Conquest of Mars." His successful career had led people to believe that he could invent anything, even devices capable of subduing whole worlds.

Prophesies and rumors aside, in public at least, Edison made it clear that his role as a wartime inventor focused on defense—not weapons of aggression. Even after a German submarine sank the British liner *Lusitania* in May 1915, killing 1,198 (including 100 Americans), Edison considered war a last resort for the United States. He also was a pragmatist. "How could we help by going into the war?" Edison argued. "We haven't any troops, we haven't any ammunition, we are an unorganized mob. I cannot believe that Germany even seriously fears our entrance."

As U.S. entanglement in the conflict seemed imminent in 1917, Edison focused more and more on the practical problem of the conduct of war. He equated technology with victory. Americans, Edison believed, were particularly well suited for modern warfare because they were excellent mechanics. "The soldier of the future," he said in 1915, "will not be a sabre-bearing, bloodthirsty savage. He will be a machinist. The war of the future, that is, if the United States engages in it, will be a war in which machines, not soldiers, fight."

While dramatizing the changing nature of warfare, Edison was not completely off the mark. The clash of forces at the Ardennes, the Marne, Ypres, and the Somme pitted countless forces against each other in limited space. But the war also saw the replacement of horses with airplanes, tanks, machine guns, mustard gas, and barbed wire.

These were the views of an individual many people believed could produce the changes he envisioned. As the debate over preparedness became heated and the chances for the United States to enter the war became less remote, Edison's stock rose as an important resource. Upon his selection to head the Naval Consulting Board in 1915, W. T. Walsh of *Illustrated World* stated, "The American public believes in miracles, in the power of sudden invention to stem national disaster. . . . The nation is now looking for just such a miracle. A little man works in a laboratory in West Orange, New Jersey. As years go, he is an old man . . . Nevertheless, this is the man the Nation has asked to take upon his shoulders the great burden of making our navy . . . efficient." Walsh added a caveat, "But the public must not be dazzled by Edison's fame. It must not expect that this great scientist can do the impossible. It can, in all probability, expect little more from him than the organization and direction of the bureau. And that is enough."

Edison was selected as president of the Naval Consulting Board precisely because many were "dazzled by his fame." In late fall 1915, for example, he and his family journeyed to San Francisco for the Panama-Pacific Exposition. "Edison Day" was held there on October 21, marking the thirty-sixth anniversary of the electric light. These celebrations were constant reminders of Edison's accomplishments—and his celebrity.

The Naval Consulting Board was an early attempt in the United States to mobilize science in wartime. However, it proved to be more important as a precedent than as a producer of concrete results. The deliberations of the board often played out controversies in the scientific community, such as the advantages of applied versus pure research, the relationship between science and technology, and the question of who should direct and control scientific inquiry. Edison was frequently a party to these debates, and brought to the board his strong preference for applied research, his wariness of college-trained scientists, and confidence in his own style of invention.

In an interview printed in the *New York Times* in May 1915, his "Plan for Preparedness" received two pages in the Sunday magazine section and spelled out his views on mechanized warfare. One particular remark caught the eye of Secretary of the Navy Josephus Daniel. "I believe," the inventor stated, "that . . . the Government should maintain a great research laboratory, jointly under military and naval and civilian control . . ."

Secretary Daniels seized the opportunity to engage the great man in his efforts to upgrade and modernize the navy. He hoped that Edison would offer advice and also employ his "magnificent facilities" at West Orange in experimental work on behalf of the navy.

But Daniels wanted more from the Wizard than his expertise. The former editor of the *Raleigh News and Observer* recognized the publicity value of Edison's name. As an advocate of strong civilian control of the navy—which piqued many top officers—enlisting Edison gave Daniels an edge in developing some of his controversial departmental reforms, especially those that "popularized technology" to support naval expansion. Also, Daniels was trying to contend with President Wilson's unshakable commitment to neutrality, which, while admirable, had stymied the preparedness program.

In a June 7 letter, Daniels asked Edison to assist in the formation of "a department of invention and development," noting that the inventor's popularity was necessary to gain support for the idea and would be an important step toward prepared-ness. Edison was quick to reply with an "Aye, Aye, Sir." After Edison agreed to serve, Daniels convinced him to march in the New York City Preparedness Parade in May 1916.

Members of the board were announced in September, and it was a telling sign of Edison's viewpoint on research in many ways. Twenty-two representatives, two each from eleven national societies selected by Edison, were invited to participate on the board. They primarily represented engineers, however. Obvious omissions included the National Academy of Science and the National Physical Society. More apparent to outsiders was the exclusion of famous inventors such as Orville Wright.

The board consisted of men with extensive practical experi-ence such as Frank J. Sprague and Elmer A. Sperry. Two mem-bers headed major industrial laboratories, and nine were company presidents. Some members, especially physicist Arthur Gordon Webster, grumbled about the lack of more scien-tists on the board. But Daniels was not inclined to protest, and Edison was happy with the emphasis on practical experience. Speaking for Edison, Miller Reese Hutchison replied to Webster that the board was composed of "*practical* men who are accus-tomed to *doing* things, and not *talking* about it."

The membership of the board by and large represented technical experts a generation removed from Edison. All but four had college degrees; some had taken advanced academic work abroad. More than half had been officers in their profes-sional societies. Even as practical men rather than theoretical sci-entists, Edison's colleagues were linked more closely to the future than the past. They represented an emphasis on speciali-zation, sophisticated industrial research, and the marriage of science and technology.

The selection of such a distinguished group met only with enthusiasm. *Literary Digest* viewed the board as worth "a million dollars or a score of battleships." *Leslie's* believed it possible for the board to "revolutionize warfare" and make the United States invulnerable to attack. *Electrical World* characterized the appointees as men of "rare inventive genius." And the editor of *Engineering Magazine* viewed the board as "the greatest thing that has ever happened in all naval and engineering annals."

The work of the group was more tedious and less dramatic than the hopes expressed in the press. The Naval Consulting Board was designed to apply the cumulative knowledge of its members to specific problems of importance to the various navy technical bureaus. Edison made it clear in his correspondence that "the board is an advisory board & not a board of invention." Initially it was assigned eighteen problems ranging from submarine detection to eliminating the rusting of equipment. To accomplish the work, the board was divided into committees.

It also played an important role in evaluating 110,000 ideas for new inventions received from the public. Only 110 met the necessary standards to be submitted to committees, and only one was put into production. The most popular devices dealt with submarines and submarine detection, ship protection, nets and shields, torpedoes, and aircraft equipment.

The major issue facing the members was Edison's idea for a research laboratory. This one issue dominated the deliberations until the board's termination. Following up on his statements in the newspaper, Edison came to the first meeting on October 7, 1915 with an outline for a facility, to be directed by a naval officer, that would be equipped for research and development as well as for limited production. The estimated start-up cost was five million dollars, with an annual budget of three million dollars. Others on the board, and the public at large, responded favorably.

Almost immediately, however, the idea was embroiled in controversy. Edison envisioned a facility that would closely resemble the West Orange Laboratory. "The proposed laboratory," as he explained sometime later, "is to build anything from a submarine to a microscope and is not a research laboratory; it is a constructing laboratory—more properly a universal machine shop—whose specialty is rapid construction by special tools and system of working." This glorified machine shop would develop prototypes of inventions leading to the mass production of goods by private industries.

Edison's navy laboratory mirrored not only West Orange but also the Wizard's perspective on invention. While he had demonstrated the potency of organized research, the new industrial research that followed placed greater stock in scientifically based team efforts as it was maturing in laboratories at Bell, Dupont, Kodak, General Electric, and on several college campuses. Since Edison did not successfully adapt to this tradition, his vision was at odds with those who were its products.

Another debate concerned administrative control. A longstanding rivalry persisted in the navy between engineers and line officers who wanted to maintain strict supervision over any new research and development facility. Bureau chiefs and line admirals also remained wary of any idea coming from civilians, in this case the Naval Consulting Board and Secretary Daniels.

Some of the brass questioned the need for the laboratory. The navy already had in place several research facilities including the Naval Torpedo Station in Newport, Rhode Island; the Naval Ordnance Proving Ground in Indianhead, Maryland; the Experimental Model Basin at the Washington Navy Yard; the Fuel Oil Test Plant in Philadelphia; and the Engineering Experiment Station at Annapolis. Proponents of the new facility argued, however, that most of the existing sites concentrated on testing. Traditionally, the navy depended on inventors and private companies for their research.

Edison did not take kindly to criticism about the laboratory. His intense determination drove him to promote the idea and see that it was funded. Yet, the array of criticisms from within the navy and without (such as *Scientific American*'s claim that it was too expensive) led the board to scale down its request for funds from $5 million to $1.5 million.

Controversy continued to dog the project. There was substantial debate over implementation. A central issue was the question of location. The initial recommendation called for the construction of the lab at Annapolis, adjacent to the Naval Academy. In the Department itself the preferred site was the District of Columbia. In both cases, proximity to existing naval facilities and to Washington was crucial.

But Edison demurred. In a minority report, he suggested Sandy Hook, New Jersey, on the northern tip of the Garden

State across the water from New York City, which provided an "unlimited amount of flat land away from inhabited places, where experiments can be made unobserved." As a location on the sea, Sandy Hook also offered "nearly practical conditions" for testing, and transportation was good. Most significantly, he envisioned Sandy Hook as strategically located to take advantage of New York City's large labor force and its availability of supplies. In a December 15, 1916, letter to Secretary Daniels, Edison stated that in New York "nearly every article sold in the United States can be found in stock. In the City and vicinity of New York is the greatest collection of factories in the Country making the most diverse articles, and all this vast variety of materials can be instantly placed at the disposal of the Laboratory." The new facility also would be—not coincidentally—close to West Orange. In essence, Edison conceived of the project within the inventive and marketing sphere he knew best (and trusted most), not within the sphere of the navy.

Rejection of his recommendation for siting the research facility at Sandy Hook raised Edison's doubts about navy control. With the board standing against him, he was making as clear a break as possible between their view and his. He expressed little confidence in Annapolis trained officers to understand scientific research or to run a laboratory. He could not see how a naval officer could avoid interference or fall under the influence of one or more bureau chiefs. "I still think that the Secretary of the Navy only should have control through civilians," he told Daniels toward the end of the war. "If Naval officers are to control it the results will be zero. This is my experience due to association with them for two years and noting the effects of the system of education at Annapolis."

Edison was transferring his personal experience about civilian leadership in research to the issue at hand. In addition, there very well may have been some lingering resentment against the navy for not following through on several of his suggestions for new devices. In one instance, the navy tested his storage batteries for use on submarines. An explosion of an E2 prototype in January 1916 resulted in the death of four men. The accident was attributed to hydrogen build-up from the batteries. The well-publicized event threatened future cooperation between Edison's companies and the navy and exposed him to some serious criticism and several lawsuits. Edison's confrontation with the navy, as one biographer observed, "pitted an irresistible inventor against an immovable bureaucracy—Edison could think only of why things should work, the admirals solely of why they wouldn't."

The majority report of the board prevailed despite Edison's efforts. While Secretary Daniels favored the majority report, he could not act without drawing the wrath of Edison. To defy the Wizard was to unravel the political advantage achieved in courting him in the first place. Daniels tried to address his dilemma in a letter to gently move Edison to accept the majority report. "I have not yet acted," he added, "solely because of my deference to you and my great confidence in your judgment." Edison was not about to change his mind, and the impasse persisted during the war.

Momentum for developing the laboratory slipped out of both Edison's and Daniels's hands after the war. In late 1919 Rear Admiral William S. Smith, who had been the navy liaison officer to the NCB, convinced the chiefs of the bureaus to advise the secretary to go ahead with the project. The site, which most officers favored, would be the District of Columbia. Daniels agreed and went ahead without Edison's consent. The contract for construction was granted in November 1920, and Edison resigned from the board in December.

The navy did not complete the facility until the middle of 1923, and it scrapped the demand for a civilian director. Admiral Smith was given the post in September 1921. Ironically, in 1952 a bust of Thomas Edison was erected at the entrance of the laboratory. By the time of his death in 1931, however, he was reconciled to the chain of events that produced the new facility. In a cordial letter to the navy he stated that his objection to the chosen location had been without foundation.

Edison was more comfortable in his workshop than in the committee room, and he sensed that he could make a greater contribution to the war effort doing what he did best. "I am not going to do a stick of work for anyone but Uncle Sam until the damned Dutchman [*sic*] is licked," Edison announced. During 1917 and 1918, while the United States was embroiled in the conflict, he devoted most of his time to naval research.

West Orange was caught up in the wartime patriotism. Many workers enlisted, but many new ones filled the ranks to produce goods for the armed forces under numerous government contracts. In all, Edison and his staff submitted more than forty plans and inventions to the navy for their consideration. Many experiments focused on submarine detection and surface ship protection. When Germany turned to unrestricted submarine warfare in 1917 to break the deadlock of trench warfare on the continent, the menace increased to critical proportions for belligerent and neutral shipping alike. Detecting submarines by sound became a major preoccupation, and Edison experimented with telephones, resonators, towing devices, and other sound equipment. While he was able to detect sounds of moving vessels as far as five thousand yards away, he was unable to perfect a towing device that would work effectively at greater distances and in anything but calm seas. Work with an outrigger listening device for detecting torpedoes was more promising, but experimentation was curtailed when the government terminated Edison's use of an old yacht for testing.

Another avenue of inquiry was less passive—limiting the ability of the submarine to view its target. In January 1918 Edison suggested that machine guns on surface vessels be used to destroy periscopes. On other occasions, he recommended smudging the skyline with black smoke to camouflage ships and laying oil on the water to blind submarines. More promising work on submarine detection was done by experts at GE and AT&T, which coupled an electronic listening device with an early radio telephone. The later development by British scientists of an active sonar system—which used reflected sound waves instead of passive listening devices—eventually moved submarine detection to a higher level of expertise.

As an alternative to submarine and torpedo detection, Edison experimented with improving surface vessel defenses. He developed "collision mats" (used to cover holes made by explosions), ten of which would cover each side of a vessel and could be rolled up before use. He developed "sea anchors" to allow cargo ships to make quick turns to avoid torpedoes. "All the Naval fellows thought I couldn't do it," he stated. "But I did it in spite of it all. It rather surprised me." He also dabbled in camouflaging, rigging ships with torpedo nets and underwater searchlights. He designed on-ship safety devices, and he studied naval maneuvers such as zigzagging.

Interestingly, Edison's major contribution came through a common-sense notion that sinkings be plotted on a map to determine where the areas of heaviest risk existed. It was clear from the research that many ships were still sailing along prewar routes, where most sinkings occurred, and were crossing this "danger zone" in daylight hours when 94 percent of the sinkings took place. "The conclusion of the Navy Dept. seemed to be, as I saw it from observing a number of officers, was your chances of hunting rabbits at night are very much increased by darkness," Edison recalled. "All the troopships were sent in the darkness . . . but as they never had any head or tail over there . . . the result was they sailed the boats according to the old sailing charts. . . . The Germans must have been astounded at the stupidity. No strategy. No brains or anything used. Fancy an army being moved that would follow the old way of doing this. . . . There they had 900 miles to run ships in, and they entered them all in about 100, and then they ran in the daytime. There is a graveyard of ships all sunk in the daytime. They could have sailed in the night." The strategic plan, plus the introduction of the convoy system in 1917 (which Edison strongly advocated), effectively contributed to reducing the submarine menace.

Despite his energy and enthusiasm for the war work, Edison received little satisfaction in his dealings with the navy. "I made about forty-five inventions during the war, and all perfectly good ones, and they pigeon-holed every one of them," he complained. "The naval officer resents any interference by civilians. Those fellows are a close corporation." The relationship was not helped by the explosion of the E2, nor by Edison's battles over the research laboratory. His casual, earthy style was foreign to the staid officers corps. It only encouraged a mutual suspicion, or at least a mutual wariness. That most of Edison's "forty-five inventions" were rather speculative, impulsively conceived, and not completely developed limited his immediate usefulness to the navy.

However, patriotic zeal and the irresistible challenge posed by the application of new technology to warfare sustained the Wizard to the very end of the conflict. He could not be accused, as some businesses were after the war, of being a "Merchant of Death." He gladly accepted contracts for his phonographs and storage batteries from the government, but his wartime research was in a separate category. In fact, since government contracts accounted for much of the work at West Orange during the war, the production of more profitable items (phonographs and dictating machines) languished.

In the end, the war was not a great boon to TAE, Inc. After the initial shock of the war temporarily broke up European markets, demand for Edison products began to improve. Even after the explosion of the E2, his storage batteries acquired wide use in radio telegraphy and on surface and sub-surface vessels. But, in general, marketing problems persisted until the 1920s. At a particularly low point in 1918, Stephen Mambert, then vice president and financial executive for TAE, Inc., confided in a letter, "The tense market conditions created by the war, which have made it so difficult to procure materials either in reasonable time or at reasonable prices, have frequently caused extreme exasperation, and perhaps sometime led to a feeling of despair regarding any relief of the pressure until the conclusion of the war."

Nonetheless, the reorganization of the Edison enterprises into Thomas A. Edison, Inc., had insured stability through the trying wartime years. Charles Edison, by then, had emerged as the new leader. With his father hot on the trail of one naval invention after another, Charles operated the various interests quite effectively. He was beginning to put his own stamp on the business and come out from the shadows of the great man. Even the Wizard recognized Charles's abilities. Quite pleased with his son's work, Edison told reporters that Charles had developed an organization "which relieves me from the details of business."

While Thomas Edison had no intention of retiring from the laboratory or the business world after the war, at the age of seventy-two he was in no position to want Charles anywhere but at the head of the family enterprise. World War I was a passage into the twilight years for Edison in the 1920s, a time when his stature as a celebrity would run well ahead of achievements as an inventor or a businessman.

CHAPTER ELEVEN

Twilight Years

A time of contrasts, an era of ultimate variety, the 1920s seemed far closer to the modern era in scope and scale than what came before World War I. "What is called Western or modern civilization by way of contrast with the civilization of the Orient or medieval times is at bottom a civilization that rests upon machinery and science as distinguished from one founded on agricultural or handicraft commerce," wrote eminent historian Charles A. Beard in 1928. "It is in reality a technological civilization."

This was the society that Thomas Edison helped to create. He was synonymous with the new mechanized and electrified world. But for Edison the man, the 1920s were not the beginning of something new. In his seventies, chronic ill health and a lifetime of hard work had finally caught up with him. His celebrity status hid his physical condition from the public.

The press continued to present the Wizard as the robust, steely-eyed, plain-talking man he had always been. But the fire inside him was dying. Edison could no longer keep up with the relentless pace of running his lab on a few hours' sleep or keeping on top of the activities of his many businesses. And maybe he did not want to. He came home for dinner more often. He slept in his own bed more often. And he regularly escaped the routine of West Orange with lengthier winter stays in Florida. He certainly had earned a rest, had earned the notoriety that his last years brought him.

He now craved the stability of family life. Mina—or "Billy" as he called her—was a loving companion. She and her husband shared few personality traits or social interests, but he thrived on her loyalty and she on his affection. A reserved person with strong religious convictions, Mina gave her time to the Methodist church and an array of religious and civic groups. She even helped to pass the New Jersey blue laws.

Mina organized home life around her husband, but balanced her own interests effectively against those of her "impatient patient one." After one uncomfortable evening when a cynical Edison verbally tangled with several of Mina's clerical guests, she did not end the practice but simply limited the number at future dinners, making talk of religion off-limits. In the 1920s more than any other time in his life, Edison needed a constant companion like Mina, and her company became more precious to him than ever before.

His relationship with his children was not as uniformly satisfying. Marion, Thomas, Jr., and William Leslie had shared life at a distance from their father and were uncomfortable with Mina. Marion, or Dot as Edison called her, was tall and pretty and possessed her father's spirit. Edison had been more affectionate with her than the boys, but she pulled away from the family when Mina entered the picture. After boarding school, she had traveled widely in Europe and eventually fell in love and then married German officer Karl Oscar Oeser. She lived in Germany for more than thirty years. Thomas and Mina met their son-in-law while traveling in Europe in 1914 or 1915 but did not see Marion again for ten years. When her marriage ended in a messy divorce, she returned to the United States for good in 1925.

Thomas, Jr., never fulfilled his father's expectations. He was fragile and sickly. Living for long periods in his aunt's Menlo Park house, he was never involved in the family routine and often found himself in trouble of one kind or another. His father had discouraged him from going to college, but he gamely tried to make it on his own as an inventor. Banking on his name, he established "Thomas A. Edison, Jr., Electric Company" and "Edison, Junior, Chemical Company," and he briefly caught the interest of Henry Ford with the development of a "period timer" for cars and trucks. Dishonest associates and poor business practices doomed the ventures. Edison, in a rather callous move, distanced himself from potential legal impediments by disowning his son. A reconciliation followed some time later, but the damage was done to the relationship. Bouts with alcohol and a bad marriage did not make Tom's life much easier. In 1936, at the age of sixty, he committed suicide.

Tom's brother Will also drifted away from the family home. Strong and athletic, he found military service an outlet for his ambitions. At twenty, he enlisted during the Spanish-American War. After recovering from yellow fever, he turned to life as "a man about town." In 1918 he joined the tank division of the American Expeditionary Force in Europe. After the war Will tried several business ventures as a civilian, including "Edison Automobile Company," but with little success. Eventually he became a gentleman farmer in New Jersey. He died of cancer in 1937, only six years after his father's death.

Life for Mina's children was substantially better. Mina was determined not to have them alienated from their father. She also insisted on providing them a strong religious upbringing and contested her husband's prejudice against formal education. Edison was living a more routine—if not entirely typical—middle-class life when his three youngest children were born. Mina's steady hand and Edison's own maturity helped to give the younger children some continuity that was missing from the lives of the three eldest children, who had suffered through the trauma of their mother's untimely death, the difficulty of life as stepchildren, and the overwhelming impact of their father's celebrity.

Madelaine, the oldest of Mina's children, resembled her father not only in appearance but in personality. She was intelligent and witty, with an earthy quality that sometimes manifested itself in salty language. More refined than her father, she attended Bryn Mawr College and spoke French. In 1914 she married John Eyre Sloane from South Orange, who ran Sloane

Aeroplane Company and School of Aviation. Marion provided her parents with their only grandchildren.

Charles, the oldest of Mina's sons and the favorite, came out from under his father's shadow more successfully than any of the other children. Mina encouraged Charles to spend time with his father, and it was not unusual to see him around the West Orange facilities. He studied at MIT but was hardly a determined student. Personable and good looking, he had better aptitude for chasing girls and playing polo than for science. However, early in his life he was being groomed (with the strong support of his mother) to take over the family business at some future date. He had enjoyed drama and poetry in school, but he earnestly set to work after he completed college in 1914. Upon the elder Edison's retirement, Charles assumed the leadership of TAE, Inc., until its sale to McGraw Electric Company in 1957. He was an effective manager, for no small reason than he got on well with his father and had confidence in himself.

Charles's personal life, in addition, was not nearly as calamitous as that of his stepbrothers. While he had ear ailments as a child, and fought the battle of the bottle as an adult, he did not succumb to the pressures of being the son of a great man. Later, Charles had a successful, if relatively brief, career in government. In 1933 he served in Franklin Roosevelt's National Recovery Administration, was appointed assistant secretary of the navy in 1937, and was secretary of the navy briefly in 1940. Later in 1940 he was elected governor of New Jersey on the New Deal coattails and served a single three-year term. He then returned to the family business and helped in its recovery from the Great Depression.

Theodore, Mina's youngest son, also experienced his father's swings from affection to indifference. "Sometimes," he recalled, "it was as if he never saw us." Theodore did extremely well in various private schools and at MIT, where he graduated in 1923. He was an excellent engineering student but wanted to become a mathematical physicist—which did not ingratiate him with his father. "Theodore is a good boy, but his forte is mathematics," Edison said. "I am a little afraid . . . he may go flying off into the clouds with that fellow Einstein. And if he does . . . I'm afraid he won't work with me."

Edison was not so much critical of Theodore as he was perplexed by him. The strong-willed lad tread too close to his father's domain. He even had his own printing press and started his own newspaper as a teenager, reminiscent of the young Al Edison. Theodore ultimately became technical director of the laboratory after his father's retirement and was eager to try his hand at invention, especially an electronic phonograph. That he was a more capable inventor than Thomas, Jr., contributed to the periodic stormy relationship between father and son.

In addition, Theodore had much more of a social conscience, or at least a different way of expressing his values, than his father. In 1947 he used half of his inheritance to establish the Edison Industries Mutual Association, an employees' trust fund. He hoped the workers would eventually assume control of the business. Later in life he became an advocate of population control and many environmental causes and was an early opponent of the Vietnam War.

To a large degree, Edison's commitment to his career had defined the relationship with his wife and children. They had always been a distant second on his list of priorities. But in the 1920s even his ability to devote himself to his career waned. Advancing age and illness were taking their toll. While Edison still could perform well for the journalists, his youthful vigor had been spent. Furthermore, he could do little to block the onrush of corporate consolidation and professional management that took his companies out of his hands. Nor could he stem the tide of modern research and development, which depended more heavily on technical specialists and scientific theory than trial and error methods. Ironically, the man who had done the most to end the tradition of the lone inventor by establishing the first major research laboratory found his own methods superseded by the systematized industrial research facilities of AT&T and Bell. Edison, alas, was becoming outmoded.

What attention he gave to his work in the 1920s largely focused on refinements of earlier inventions, most especially the phonograph as well as business machines and the storage battery. For whatever reason—stubbornness, stodginess, or a growing conservatism—he took little interest in the emerging field of electronics, a field he helped to set in motion with the discovery of the "etheric force." He dismissed the commercialization of radio—"The present radio . . . is certainly a lemon . . ."—and he continued to tinker with mechanical phonographs despite the Bell laboratory's development of an electronic phonograph. Charles and Theodore begged their father to test new ideas, but to little avail. Ultimately, they were forced to work on projects behind his back. "My father's past experience," Theodore concluded, "had simply got in his way."

The West Orange facility, in general, was changing in the 1920s. Stephen Mambert favored financial results over long-term projects or the various jobs conducted for Edison's personal interest. The Phonograph Works was the major customer, and the work of the machine shops and engineering services supported the manufacture of phonographs. The laboratory also served as a central testing facility for the various manufacturing activities. Laboratory procedure was quite orderly, but it was so closely controlled that the professional engineers could not carry out their own research.

Edison never stopped tinkering but withdrew from the day-to-day routine. Increasingly, he worked in his Fort Myers center and in a room at Glenmont. The transformation of the West Orange facility itself also proved to be uncomfortable for him. The major effort to rationalize the laboratory meant that all major experiments needed prior approval of the company's board. Amazingly, and sadly, the board refused to pay for some of Edison's experiments, and he was forced to use his personal resources to carry on pet projects. Business was business.

The "squeeze" seemed reminiscent of his disengagement from GE several years before, but more precisely it reflected an important transition in industrial research of which Edison was no longer a leading figure. While the work was more orderly under the new regime, it was also much more routine—hardly the environment in which Edison had operated best, and one in which he saw little chance for innovation.

More bewildering was his growing resistance to the needs of the marketplace. Edison had been a pioneer in transforming inventions into products for mass consumers. He periodically underestimated the potential of some inventions, but he eventually came around to taking advantage of opportunities initiated by others. While he finally accepted the inevitability of the disc phonograph, he resisted broadening the list of record titles to meet consumer tastes and demand. The perfection of the machine's fidelity seemed more important than sales. Although he had always placed great stock in the quality of his products, he seemed to care less about marketability as he moved farther away from the business affairs of his companies.

This was particularly true with the phonograph. By 1925 radio dominated the entertainment market and was changing musical tastes. Customers responded favorably to the loudness and enhanced bass notes possible through electrical amplification. But Edison responded to the challenge of "radio sound" not by direct competition but by improving the tone of the disc and by developing a long-playing record. His competitor, Victor, confronted the radio challenge more effectively by adopting a system of electrical recording. Within a short time, Victor led the way in replacing the acoustic phonograph with the high-fidelity phonograph.

Because TAE, Inc., had five different product lines—business and amusement phonographs, primary and storage batteries, and cement—it was able to survive the problems of any one product and other business dislocations. And the West Orange laboratory, despite having lost its leadership role, remained an important research facility. But it was not the force of innovation that characterized Edison's laboratory in the nineteenth and early twentieth centuries.

In 1928 Edison Phonograph Works brought out an electronic phonograph—its last new product—and began to market radio receivers. Others, namely Radio Company of America (formed by GE and AT&T who had pooled their radio patents in

1919), came to dominate radio by the time TAE, Inc., got into the market. After losing almost two million dollars, the company pulled out. It met a similar fate in the marketing of the Edicraft range of electrical appliances. The picture of the inventor on the toasters and coffee makers was not enough to overcome the steep decline in consumer demand with the onset of the Great Depression.

Edison's rubber experiments in the 1920s were his "last campaign," harkening back to the inventor of old. The need for vast amounts of rubber by the growing automobile industry spurred Edison to find an alternative to natural rubber from Malaya, Ceylon, Africa, and Brazil. He first became interested in rubber during his 1915 visit with botanist Luther Burbank in California. Edison had duly noted the need for rubber in wartime. After the price of rubber skyrocketed in 1924 and 1925, Henry Ford and Harvey Firestone uged Edison to seek new sources and agreed to finance the operation. Edison Botanic Research Company was established in 1927. With a renewed vigor, Edison poured himself into the project, which was much like his earlier ventures in its demand for an empirical approach. He collected a vast library of pertinent sources, sent representatives out in search of usable materials, and after testing almost fourteen thousand plants, deemed the domestic goldenrod the most promising. Through crossbreeding he developed a fourteen-foot monster. The first rubber extracted showed potential but was years away from being commercially viable. Time was running out on the Wizard, however, and he became too ill in the last years of the decade to give the project his full attention.

He had achieved celebrity status. His heightened notoriety was an additional reason for his lack of productivity in the 1920s. Edison always had been quotable and he certainly received his due—perhaps more—in the press, among world leaders, and in the public. He was one of those rare individuals who did not have to die to become famous.

The Edison legend was reinforced with every monument, medal, decoration, and honor bestowed on him in these years. Delegations flocked to Glenmont and other sites to view the great man. These were opportunities for Edison to expound on every conceivable subject—a practice he rarely avoided. In discussing future urban life, he told a reporter from *Forum Magazine* that the mathematician would supplant the traffic policeman in the modern city by solving the problem of traffic congestion; that modern urbanites would be sufficiently deafened by nature to withstand the increased din of the metropolis.

He had opinions on every social issue. On Prohibition he noted, "You hear talk about restriction of personal liberty in speaking about Prohibition. What is civilization but restriction of personal liberty for the improvement of mankind?" On matters religious, he proved to be an agnostic. Mysticism fascinated him more than his wife's fundamentalism. And he was more insistent that children be taught facts and exposed to theories than to be lectured to on the Bible. On politics, he voiced a steady cynicism. Asked in a questionnaire in 1923, "The American people have lost confidence in their political leaders. Why?" he replied, "I can't remember that they ever had very much."

For every question, on almost any subject, he had an answer. Question: "If the population of the world continues to increase at the rate of the past half century, what will be the result in 200 years?" Answer: "War." Question: "Comparing the electrical industry with the life of a human being . . . at what stage of life do you think it now stands?" Answer: "Yelling baby." Much of the time Edison simply shot from the hip or gave reporters something to quote rather than offering an insight.

Renown meant hobnobbing with other celebrities. But real friends were in short supply. The death of Batchelor and other "muckers" left Edison alone in the laboratory. The estrangement of Hutchison whittled away at the few trusted associates he had made over the years. Thus his friendship with automobile legend Henry Ford in the 1910s and the 1920s represented more than photo opportunities for the press.

For Ford the relationship was hero worship pure and simple. On February 18, 1907, a year before the marketing of the Model T, Ford wrote to Edison:

> My Dear Mr. Edison:
>   I am fitting up a den for my own private use at the factory and I thought I would like to have photographs of about three of the greatest inventors of this age to feast my eyes on in idle moments. Needless to say Mr. Edison is the first of the three and I would esteem it a great personal favor if you would send me a photograph of yourself.
>
>   Very sincerely yours,
>   Henry Ford

Ford received no answer to his query, nor did Edison seem to recall a couple of chance meetings with the soon-to-be Flivver King in the years before his name became a household word. Ford, however, cherished the memory of every encounter.

At the concluding banquet of the 1896 convention of the Association of Edison Illuminating Companies, Ford got a chance to discuss his gasoline-powered vehicle with the great man. Edison was quite interested in the animated discussion of the budding carmaker and asked him numerous questions. At one point Edison pounded the table and asserted, "Young man, that's the thing! You have it!—the self-contained unit carrying its own fuel with it. Keep at it." Ford thrived on the inspiration of that meeting and on the hope of more in the future. "The bang on the table," Ford later recalled, "was worth worlds to me."

In times past, Edison had shunned or ignored innovative rivals—Bell, Sprague, Dickson, Westinghouse, Tesla—threatened by their competition or suspicious of their motives. Why not Ford? Was it because Ford was working in a discrete field far enough removed from Edison's own interests? Probably not—he believed that all technology was his backyard. Was it because he enjoyed Ford's hero worship? Not likely. Edison did not need such outpourings to feel confident about his own work. More likely Edison befriended the young inventor because Ford was a link with his past. They shared many childhood experiences and held common values.

While Edison was more protean and more imaginative than the younger Ford, he was comfortable with Ford's commonality, his love for machines, his desire for tangible accomplishments. And he admired Ford's achievements in the rough world of business. In an earlier time Edison would have been threatened by Ford's success; in his twilight years those successes were reminders of his own exploits.

As a fervent admirer of the Wizard, Ford placed few demands on Edison save to keep the great inventor's legacy in the public gaze, not to upstage it. This was a relationship quite essential to Edison as he moved away from active life to the role of a legend. Most emphatically, he saw the legacy of his individualistic style sustained in the coming generations through Henry Ford.

In the 1930s (after Edison's death), Mexican artist Diego Rivera created a fresco for the Detroit Institute of Arts depicting the faces of Edison and Ford in a superimposed image, blending the portraits of the two men into one figure. The symbolism of these "makers of the twentieth century" intertwined as a single force for material progress expressed the common roots and the common beliefs held by these men that bound them together in a special way.

Ford's father, William, had emigrated to the United States from Ireland in 1847, the year Edison was born. William and his wife Mary started a farm in Michigan, where Henry—the first child—was born in 1863. Sharing Michigan roots with Edison in his childhood, Ford also gave little time to formal education, loved to tinker with machinery, had a father who questioned his potential, and had a warm and loving relationship with his mother. Mary died in childbirth in 1876 when Henry was twelve. He was devastated and believed that "a great wrong" had been done to him by losing the one person who encouraged his natural abilities. Edison had felt the same loss when Nancy died.

Like Edison, Ford turned to the city for opportunity. In 1879 he went to Detroit—the same city Edison had first experienced. Although Ford returned regularly to Dearborn to help with the harvest, he gained valuable experience in Detroit, first in a shop that repaired steam engines and then as a repairman of watches and clocks. He soon apprenticed at Flower Brothers' machine shop and, at the age of seventeen, became a journeyman machinist with the Detroit Drydock Company. In 1891 he went to work for Detroit Edison Company and ran the power station so efficiently that he had time to set up a private workshop in some unused space. He quickly became an advocate of DC power, believing it more efficient than the rival AC power.

For a time, Ford returned to the country, working as a fix-it man and itinerant serviceman. His ambitions and his love for machines led him into the automobile business. He built his first experimental car in 1896 while working at Detroit Edison. He made two unsuccessful attempts to enter the highly competitive new industry. At the age of forty, he formed Ford Motor Company in Detroit in June 1903 with new backers. In 1908 he introduced the Model T—the first successful mass-produced gasoline automobile—which embodied the crucial qualities of simplicity, plainness, and dependability. The Model T was wildly successful, and Ford's innovative assembly line techniques set off a revolution in industrial production. After the 1920s, one could no longer think of America and not think of the automobile. Nor could one forget the accomplishments of Henry Ford, who, as a result of his breakthrough, became the first billionaire through a company which he alone owned and controlled.

Ford became a folk hero in his own right with a genius for machinery, a sense of order, a faith in technology, and an unswerving adherence to national advancement. Sometimes these traits were inverted, however, and the unattractive side of the Flivver King emerged. A man of simple tastes, often kind and generous, his habits of denial and his sense of morality made him an opponent of personal indulgences such as smoking, and a critic of urban life. In business, he was anti-union and paternalistic. Petty and often obtuse, he was intolerant of those who failed to share his vision of the future or his interpretation of the past. What appear as paradoxes in Henry Ford's personal-

ity may be no more than characteristics of the self-made man
who achieved wealth and power before wisdom and education.

Edison not only shared a common youth but held many
beliefs with his friend Henry Ford. Edison certainly had
become more worldly than Ford, possessed no deep abiding
disdain for city life, and was much more gregarious. Edison had
an assuredness that made some of his ideas no less outrageous
than Ford's but made them appear less vindictive, less defen-
sive, and more palatable. While opinionated, Edison also was
far less intolerant of new ideas than Ford. The two men shared
the broad outlines of a world view that incorporated ardor for
progress through technology, a disdain for elitism, and an
almost nostalgic perception of nineteenth-century individualism and hard work.

The industrial world had been good to both men; they had
made their mark on the world through the production of goods
for the mass market. What one writer said of Edison was equally
applicable to Ford, "His test of success was frankly material."
Both accepted the capitalist system as it evolved in the late nineteenth and early twentieth centuries. They held contempt for
Wall Streeters and bankers because they produced no tangible
product. They disliked unionism because it placed too much
emphasis on the workers and not enough on the means of production. In a letter to tire manufacturer Harvey Firestone in
1919, Edison noted, "You are right about the Union. I would
quit before they would ever get a chance to ruin my business.
Their leaders seem in most cases to be poor types of mental
roughnecks." When Ford announced that he was going to institute a five-dollar day for his workers—revolutionary in its scale
of pay but meant to maintain control over the work force—
Edison remarked that labor unions now were "done for."

While enamored of technology as a positive force for
change, Edison and Ford shared a wariness of professional scientists and technical experts. In practice, however, both men
came to depend upon experts in their businesses. While Ford
avoided scientific organizations, he regularly sought the advice
of scientists and respected their expertise. Despite his public

protestations, Edison hired many specialists to work on a wide array of inventions. He just could not bring himself to admit publicly that his own self-training may have been inadequate for the knottiest problems of the laboratory. Here is where Edison's ego was most severely tested.

Neither Ford nor Edison could shake their Midwestern roots or their nineteenth-century values, although Edison was much less the rustic than his friend. He maintained great faith in the powers of the individual and resisted social or political pressures that sought to undermine individual rights, but he did not bristle at the evils of the city in the way Ford did. A bit of a free thinker, Edison had little time for religion. Ford, however, would never allow anyone to question his religious values, but in practice he was more preoccupied with the world of work than with the world of the spirit.

A most telling issue, anti-Semitism, embodied the worst instincts of Henry Ford and threatened to diminish Edison's reputation as well. The most widespread, and certainly the most scurrilous, attacks on Jews came in a series of 1920 articles on the "International Jew" in the *Dearborn Independent*, the house organ for the Ford Motor Company. Carried out by the editor and personal secretary to Ford, Ernest G. Liebold, the articles charged "international Jewish banking power" with starting World War I and blamed Jews for plotting to destroy "Christian civilization." Public protests and several lawsuits forced Ford to retract the charges made in his newspaper. But the damage was done, and Ford came off as an ignoramus if not a bigot.

In trying to understand the roots of Ford's blind prejudice, several influences seem credible. Civil rights was hardly an issue of public concern in the early twentieth century, and exclusionary laws and restrictive behavior affected Jews, Catholics, immigrants, blacks, and others outside the mainstream. In the parochial environment in which Ford grew up, prejudice of older stock Americans for new Americans was particularly exaggerated. In addition, Ford's limited formal education, his narrow focus on his business goals, and his lack of inquisitiveness about other cultures and many social issues was exposed in a lack of sensitivity to large groups of people of whom he knew little.

Edison cannot be blamed either for encouraging Ford to act as he did or for not effectively counseling Ford to cease and desist. However, he harbored his own prejudices that grew out of the same influences that moved Ford—that is, chronic insensitivity to racial and religious issues in the era in which they lived and the impact of their provincial backgrounds. Edison's anti-Semitic opinions showed him all too ready to accept broad stereotypes. Jews, he believed, had been largely responsible for Germany's business success that made the "Hun" a formidable enemy in World War I. He claimed that this comment was in praise of the ability of Jews, not meant to suggest that they had started the war. But at the very least he was spreading an unsubstantiated rumor.

Even in praise of Jews, Edison displayed unfortunate stereotyping. In response to one letter from a Jewish associate, he stated that Jews were certainly remarkable people "as strange to me in their isolation from all the rest of mankind, as those mysterious people called gypsies. While there are some 'terrible examples' in mercantile pursuits, the moment they get into art, music & science & Literature the jew is fine. The trouble with the jew is that he has been persecuted for centuries by ignorant malignant bigots & forced into his present characteristics and he has acquired a 6th sense which gives him almost unerring judgement in trade affairs." Unfortunately, celebrity status granted men like Ford and Edison a forum to discuss many issues which they were often not qualified to deal with.

The compatibility of Edison and Ford brought them together throughout the latter years of Edison's life. They became involved in some business deals, as in the case of Edison supplying batteries for Ford's cars. However, joint business ventures were a very small part of their relationship, except when Ford provided financial support for new projects.

The best known of their encounters were a series of camping trips or "gypsy tours." During his 1915 trip to California to attend the Panama-Pacific Exposition, Edison found touring in an open automobile to be a "splendid distraction." He subsequently made plans with Ford, Harvey Firestone, and naturalist John Burroughs to go on an extended camping trip once they returned home. Burrough's embrace of the wonders of the outdoors appealed to nature-lover Ford, while the sense of adventure captivated Edison. Burroughs proved an excellent addition to the group because, as Edison noted in 1921, "Burrough's wide knowledge, his thorough understanding of a thousand and one interesting things in life, made him a wonderful companion and friend."

The first tour took place in the summer of 1916, sans Ford who was preoccupied with business. The one-thousand-mile trip extended from New Jersey to Vermont. A second and much more elaborate tour through the Shenandoah Valley and into the Great Smokies was undertaken in 1918—this time with Ford in attendance.

The gypsy business magnates and their friends hardly "roughed it," eating off of china plates, attended by servants, and fawned over by the press. Ford liked the coverage and scurried around chopping wood and generally enjoying the recreation that the trip provided. Edison, having lived most of his adult life in the city, relished meditating and reading in his temporary journey back to nature.

Other trips followed, with the last one in 1924. By that time wives were invited along, and celebrities such as presidents Harding, Coolidge, and Hoover visited the campsites. Burroughs had died in 1921, and Edison was becoming infirm. The joy of "shaking-up" along the bumpy roads was losing its charm. Subsequent reunions were held at Fort Myers.

The images that the camping trips conjured were marvelous public relations episodes. Here were several of the most powerful men in the world dressing in shirt sleeves, hiking, sitting around a campfire, and generally relaxing. They had been completely taken out of the context in which people visualized them and thus were made a little more human.

One apocryphal story—told in several versions—summarized the local impact of these "Five Wizards in the Wilds" as they traveled across the countryside. Apparently the car carrying Ford, Edison, and Burroughs broke down in the mountains of West Virginia. A village mechanic assessed the damage and declared that the trouble was in the motor. "I am Henry Ford," one of the passengers said, "and I say the motor is running perfectly." The mechanic then suggested that the problem was electrical. "I am Thomas A. Edison," another passenger announced, "and I say the wiring is all right." At this point the mechanic turned to the snow-white-bearded Burrough and said, "And I suppose that must Santa Claus."

The camping trips made for good stories in the press and revealed the substantial change in Edison's life after World War I. The intensity of the earlier years was gone, and celebrity fit him well. Man was becoming monument. Even in most of his public activities with Ford, Edison tended to play a supporting role, although he liked to give the illusion that his work habits and business interests had not changed.

For his part, Ford's ventures outside automobile production diminished rather than enhanced his stature. He unsuccessfully attempted to run for national office, but as Edison noted, "He is a remarkable man in one sense, and in another he is not. I would not vote for him for President, but as a director of manufacturing or industrial enterprises I'd vote for him—twice." In World War I, in an effort to persuade the belligerents to stop fighting, Ford attempted to send a "Peace Ship" to Europe in 1915. A strong pacifist, he could not convince Edison—or many other famous people—to make the journey. Supposedly Ford shouted in Edison's lifeless ears, "I'll give you a million dollars if you'll come," but Edison was only willing to give public support to his friend's rather hollow gesture toward peace—not stake his reputation on it.

After the war, Ford had tried to purchase the power sites and federally developed nitrate plants at Muscle Shoals along the Tennessee River. The bid attracted wide support from Secretary of Commerce Herbert Hoover, some southern politicians, local developers, and Thomas Edison. But Senator George Norris of Nebraska, southern power companies, and southern manufacturers, skeptical of Ford's motives, opposed it. Locally, the distaste for land speculators reinforced the notion that the

Ford offer was exploitative. Some opponents simply held a grudge against Ford. His anti-Semitism and other crude opinions also weighed into the equation. As a result of the groundswell of opposition and erosion of support, Ford withdrew his offer in 1924, saying, "A single affair of Business which should have been decided by anyone within a week has become a complicated political affair."

Edison had schooled Ford in the significance of power generation, and this certainly had influenced Ford's efforts to acquire Muscle Shoals. But Edison had his own problems growing out of the controversy. He had supported Ford's proposal to finance Muscle Shoals with an issue of paper money—"energy dollars." This led Edison to attack the gold standard—"a relic of Julius Caesar"—claiming that the issuance of paper money would eliminate Wall Street profits from bond sales and neutralize the power of gold which, he and Ford believed, was—as one reporter noted—"the chief agency causing wars." This issue also gave Edison an opportunity to criticize the concept of interest—"an invention of Satan"—and to vent other criticisms of the prevalent financial system. Muscle Shoals proved to be dangerous waters for Ford and Edison, who were both criticized severely in the press. Again, taking up the role as instant expert proved demeaning to Edison.

Public pronouncements on endless subjects and jaunts in the countryside were expressions of a career winding down. Edison seemed to enjoy his "retirement," but he had little choice given his advancing age and physical condition.

In recognition of Edison's accomplishments and in an effort to keep alive the spirit of the man he so admired, Ford set out to enshrine the memory of Edison through preserving the physical embodiment of his inventive genius—Menlo Park. Since most of the buildings had been demolished, Ford reconstructed the "invention factory" at Greenfield Village, a gigantic living museum that paid tribute to America's past and especially to industry and invention, which he strongly identified with Edison.

This preoccupation was for Ford, now in his sixties, as significant a venture as his automobile empire. Beyond his own birthplace and personal mementos of his youth, he also brought Luther Burbank's garden office, an Illinois courthouse where Lincoln had practiced law, the Wright Brothers' and Noah Webster's homes, and much, much more. This was not a museum in any classical sense, for it had dislodged objects and buildings from their original setting and placed them in a strange juxtaposition to each other. Greenfield Village was an expression of Ford's image of America, as if it were an abstract painting that changed the form but not the essence of the subject.

In a stroke of good timing, Ford decided to combine the opening of the Ford Museum and Greenfield Village with "Light's Golden Jubilee," the fiftieth anniversary of Edison's electric light, to take place in October 1929. The Edison Pioneers, a group composed of Edison's old associates, helped Ford to rescue the jubilee from the clutches of General Electric Company, which they believed would stage the event for commercial purposes. No one had bothered to consult the Old Man in all this, but Ford quickly moved ahead with his plans when a compromise was worked out with GE. There would be a joint celebration, but the main activity would take place in Dearborn. Edison agreed, and Ford set out to make preparations. Like an Egyptian pharaoh, he ordered the construction of a replica of Independence Hall in Philadelphia, which was to serve as the central museum building and the primary site for the celebration.

When Edison stepped off the train in Dearborn prior to the event, he gazed upon a part of his life that must have seemed like yesterday instead of fifty years in the past. The Menlo Park recreation had all the old bulbs and paraphernalia of those crude but exciting beginnings. There too was the railroad station at Smith's Creek, Michigan, where he had worked as a boy, and a reconstruction of the baggage car with his chemistry laboratory. Ford had not recreated Edison's entire past but only the memories that were most vividly becoming part of the folklore of the Wizard. It was as if Edison were being presented the kind of immortality that screens out all but the best recollections.

On the evening of October 21, 1929, Edison sat on display in the Menlo Park recreation to demonstrate his most famous achievement but this time in front of President Herbert Hoover, assembled dignitaries, famous scientists and inventors, and a smattering of the few remaining colleagues from years past. The model of the old carbon filament lamp was turned on. News of the event was sent over more than one hundred forty affiliates of the National Broadcasting Company, eavesdropping on a moment recalled only by the most elderly in the audience. And at the proper time an announcer with excitement in his voice declared: "And Edison said: 'Let there be light!'"

CHAPTER TWELVE

Legacy

❖
❖

The culmination of Light's Golden Jubilee was a banquet held in Edison's honor in the newly constructed replica of Independence Hall in Greenfield Village. Upon entering the hall for dinner, Edison nearly collapsed. "I won't go in," he told Mina. Having just recovered from penumonia and worn out by the events of the day, Edison had had enough of being a celebrity for a while.

Mina gave him some warm milk and coaxed him to attend the function. After all, there were five hundred well-chosen guests in attendance, including President Herbert Hoover; notable entrepreneurs John D. Rockefeller, Jr., George Eastman, Samuel Insull, Harvey Firestone, Walter P. Chrysler, Charles Nash, R.E. Olds, and Henry Ford; social activist Jane Addams; fellow inventors and scientists Marie Curie, Lee DeForest, Arthur Compton, the Mayo Brothers, and Orville Wright; and even Will Rogers.

Whether he liked it or not, Edison—seated in the place of honor vacated by President Hoover—had to receive the congratulatory letters from around the world and accept the adulation of the assembled body. Time had caught up with him. He ate nothing, sat weakly in his chair, and when called upon, read a brief speech written for him by his son Charles. Thanking Ford for his efforts, he graciously noted that in honoring him the well-wishers were also honoring "that vast army of thinkers and workers of the past and those who will carry on" without whom his work "would have gone for nothing." "The experience makes me realize as never before," he added, "that Americans are sentimental, and this great event, Light's Golden Jubilee, fills me with gratitude."

Light's Golden Jubilee demonstrated that Edison had reached the status of a legend. A publication put out by the National Electric Light Association, in conjunction with the anniversary of the electric light, suggested ways for local communities to pay tribute to Edison. Schedule main events, they suggested, shoot off fireworks, organize pageants and parades, hold receptions and educate the young. In the back of the guide was a list of merchandise available for purchase—replicas of the first lamp, reprints of the 1879 *New York Herald,* an official jubilee book, souvenir flashlights, and an array of plaques, posters, stickers, and matchbooks with Edison's picture on them. The legend had also become a consumable product.

The tribute in Dearborn was the beginning of the end for Edison. That same October in 1929 saw the stock market crash that brought to public attention the onset of the Great Depression. The heady years of the 1920s were over, and Mr. Hoover and the rest of the nation—although they could not foresee it—would face a decade and a half of economic hardship and war.

Edison had little opportunity to put his time and talents to the great problems that lay ahead. Had he been a vigorous young man he certainly would have tried to harness technology to find a solution to the mess of the 1930s. But he had begun to fail badly in 1929. And for the next two years he merely hung on to life. He visited his lab and factories less often, working instead in a room in Glenmont.

Mina tried to comfort him, and she and the children—with no illusions about what was happening—did what they could. An electric air conditioner was installed in his bedroom to make the hours pass more easily. It was a gesture out of helplessness to ease his remaining hours, not to prolong them.

On August 1, 1931, everyone braced themselves as Edison collapsed again. The doctors gave him a few days. He was diagnosed as having diabetes, uremic poisoning, Bright's disease, and an array of other maladies. He fought back and proved the doctors wrong again. But he suffered a relapse in September and passed into a coma in October. He died early Sunday morning on October 18.

During the deathwatch more than fifty newspaper reporters and assorted curiosity seekers, faith healers, and cranks milled around the Glenmont estate—almost convinced that the Wizard would find a way of solving this one last insurmountable problem. But he could not. His body was laid in state at West Orange for two days, where thousands passed by for a final glimpse. Although hardly a religious man, he had no control over the proper Christian funeral and burial upon which Mina insisted.

After his death, Mina's impulse was to flood the country with memorials to Thomas Edison, but the idea seemed ostentatious to many in the Depression years. The eulogies to Edison, nonetheless, were numerous and glowing. The response of the *Miami News* was typical, "Edison was the genius of his hour. His hour consisted of the period of 60 years into which has been crowded more mechanical invention than any previous 10 centuries produced." Friend Ford stated the profound impact of Edison's life: "His fame, his independence of the fluctuating judgments of history, his life, all are etched in light and sound on the daily and hourly life of the world." On a more personal level, Ford reflected that "Edison was the chief hero of my boyhood and he became my friend in manhood. That is a rare experience—to have one's hero for one's later friend."

Certainly the most bizarre but telling tribute came from the Guatama Buddha, "the Supreme Commander of the Entire Universe." (Exactly when the tribute was made is open to question.) Among his list of twelve Supreme Commanders of his Celestial Lodge were J.P. Morgan, in charge of "Money Securities and Real Properties"; Herbert Hoover, responsible for "Merchandising"; Henry Ford, "Raw to Finished"; Jesus Christ, "Instruction"; and Thomas Edison, "Power, Electricity, New Creation."

While the Guatama Buddha bestowed on Edison the high honor of responsibility for New Creation, columnist Walter Lippmann was more realistic in capturing his accomplishments in life. "It is impossible," Lippmann noted, "to measure the importance of Edison by adding up the specific inventions with which his name is associated. Far-reaching as many of them have been in their effect upon modern civilization, the total effect of Edison's career surpasses the sum of all of them."

It was difficult not to measure Edison by enumerating his finite accomplishments—1093 patents and a central role in the communications, transportation, and lighting and power revolutions of his time. Eschewing formal education, he accumulated an armful of honorary degrees, including a Doctor of Science from Princeton in 1915. He was awarded the Legion of Honor in France (1879), the Cross of Grand Officer in Italy (1889), the Albert Medal of the British Society of Arts (1892), the Rathenau Gold Medal in Germany (1915), and numerous awards in his own country, including the Medal of the Franklin Institute (1915) and the Congressional Gold Medal (1928).

What honors and awards did not accomplish, myth making did. The momentum of his long career made it difficult for the public not to equate the process of invention with the Wizard of Menlo Park. If Edison had not invented it, it must not exist.

While Edison could be prickly and crude, showing flashes of anti-Semitism and chauvinism about his country, exhibiting the typical traits of a Victorian male, and overworking and underpaying his workers, the whole—as Lippmann stated—was greater than the sum of the parts. His strongest traits—curiosity, practicality, perseverance, resilience—were the characteristics of a self-confident man with few delusions. In many ways he applied nineteenth-century individualism to the twentieth-century world with little modification. As a young, struggling inventor, such self-reliance was an asset. Only in his later years, as the world changed and turned to the specialist rather than the generalist, did his peers seem to pass him by. What was wizardry in the 1880s had become commonplace in the 1920s. By that time, however, his reputation preserved his accomplishments. In paying tribute to Edison on the evening of Light's Golden Jubilee, Albert Einstein stated it best, "You are equally successful as a pioneer, a developer and an organizer."

Ironically, the inventor who so masterfully demonstrated that individual effort matters found his greatest successes in the teeming cities of the Northeast. His work on the urban telegraph not only launched his career as an inventor, but sustained it as he applied the form and principles of the telegraph to his work on the telephone, the phonograph, the incandescent light, and motion pictures. The cities nurtured him and inspired him, giving his inventions definition and purpose, and in some instances even limiting his vision—as in the case of DC power. As a market for his innovations, the cities provided the financial wherewithal to push ahead to new inventions, to suggest new public needs and public wants, to serve as a foundation for building a research and manufacturing empire rivalling Edison's former benefactors in the world of business and finance. More than a backdrop for his career, the industrial city was an essential component.

Edison left the world with a legacy of invention that helped to create the twentieth century as we know it. The business of invention was likewise very good to him as he grew from a small-time entrepreneur to a major industrialist. In many ways, however, it was the intangibles of his career, those forces that drove him from accomplishment to accomplishment, that people remember. In one of several statements that he made about educating the young, Edison focused on a central ingredient of his own success, "The most necessary task of civilization is to teach men how to think."

A Note on the Sources

Thomas Edison not only left a legacy of important inventions but a wealth of documents as well. The most important depository is the Edison Archives at the Edison National Historic Site in West Orange, New Jersey, containing approximately 3.5 million items, including correspondence, memoranda, laboratory notebooks, legal files, business records, Edison's personal library, photographs, and sound recordings. Special collections include the papers of Charles Batchelor, the Motion Picture Patents Company, and the Naval Consulting Board. There are also many examples of Edison's inventions located throughout the site.

Fortunately, many of the documents only accessible to researchers until recently are being included in *Thomas A. Edison Papers: A Selective Microfilm Edition*, edited by Reese V. Jenkins. The twenty-year project will result in a six-part collection, two of which are completed. *Part I, 1850–1878* (Frederick, Md., 1985) includes patents, notebooks, litigation, document files, accounts, scrapbooks, and letterbooks. Ninety percent of the documents from that period were filmed. *Part II, 1879–1886* (Frederick, Md., 1987) emphasizes technical and business developments of the electric lighting system and includes approximately 60 percent of the documents of the period. Both sets have accompanying published guides. Also available is Jenkins, ed., *The Papers of Thomas A. Edison*, Vol. 1: *The Making of An Inventor, February 1847–June 1873* (Baltimore, 1989), which includes an excellent narrative of Edison's early life and many useful annotations accompanying the documents.

A second important cache of documents is located in the Thomas A. Edison Collection, Archives and Library Department, Henry Ford Museum and Greenfield Village, Dearborn, Michigan. These documents complement those at West Orange and include correspondence, notes, sketches, various agreements, and company brochures. Of particular note is the Edison Pioneers Collection which includes biographical information and reminiscences of individuals associated with Edison. The Edison Institute Archives, also located at the Ford Museum, includes some useful information on the acquisition and development of the Menlo Park complex at Greenfield Village and on Light's Golden Jubilee. Also of value are the Records of the U.S. Patent Office (Record Group 241) in the National Archives, Washington, D.C.

Aside from his notebooks, his penciled comments on incoming correspondence, and interviews with journalists, Edison left few private reminiscences. Either Dagobert D. Runes, ed., *The Diary and Sundry Observations of Thomas Alva Edison* (New York, 1948), or Kathleen L. McGuirk, ed., *The Diary of Thomas A. Edison* (Old Greenwich, Conn., 1970), offer a few brief glimpses of Edison's thoughts on his childhood, his deafness, education, and on the inventive process. Useful are various memoirs and reminiscences left by associates. The best known is Francis Jehl's three-volume work, *Menlo Park Reminiscences* (Dearborn, 1937). See also T. Commerford Martin, *Forty Years of Edison Service, 1882–1922* (New York, 1922); and Henry Ford and Samuel Crowther, *My Friend Mr. Edison* (London, 1930), which offers more insight about Ford's hero worship of Edison than about the inventor. Walter L. Welch's *Charles Batchelor: Edison's Chief Partner* (Syracuse, 1972), tries to elevate Batchelor to co-inventor with Edison.

Edison biographies are plentiful. Matthew Josephson's *Edison: A Biography* (New York, 1959), has been a standard among the more recent biographies. Josephson repeats many of the well-known anecdotes of Edison's life, but he also offers an image of Edison as a practical inventor. Robert Conot's *Thomas A. Edison: A Streak of Luck* (New York, 1979), is rich in detail and offers several provocative interpretations, but it lacks the coherence of Josephson's study. Wyn Wachhorst's *Thomas Alva Edison: An American Myth* (Cambridge, Mass., 1981), examines, as the dust jacket suggests, "the transmutations of Edison's image in the eyes of his countrymen as the ideal embodiment of American values and virtues . . ." A less successful effort in dealing with the Edison image and myth is David E. Nye, *The Invented Self: An Anti-biography, from Documents of Thomas A. Edison* (Odense, Denmark, 1983). See also Ronald W. Clark's popular biography, *Edison: The Man Who Made the Future* (New York, 1977).

For an extensive list of the earlier biographies, see Wachhorst, *Thomas Alva Edison*. The most important of these is Frank Lewis Dyer, Thomas Commerford Martin, and William Henry Meadowcroft, *Edison: His Life and Inventions* 2 vols. (New York, 1929), which captures Edison's own view of his accomplishments.

Useful brief accounts include Thomas P. Hughes, "Thomas Alva Edison and the Rise of Electricity," in Carroll W. Pursell, Jr., ed., *Technology in America* (Cambridge, Mass., 1981): 117–28; Reese V. Jenkins and Paul B. Israel, "Thomas A. Edison: Flamboyant Inventor," *IEEE Spectrum* 21 (December, 1984): 74–79; and Harold Livesay, "The Most Useful American, Thomas A. Edison," in Livesay, *American Made: Men Who Shaped the American Economy* (Boston, 1979): 127–56. For an exotic twist on Edison's childhood, see Juan Cuitlahuac de Hoyos, "Inquiries into Thomas Alva Edison's Alleged Mexican Ancestry," *Aztlan* 9 (1978): 151–76.

Understanding Edison's method as an inventor is crucial to appreciating his accomplishments. See Thomas P. Hughes, "Edison's Method," in William P. Pickett, ed., *Technology at the Turning Point* (San Francisco, 1977): 5–22; Hughes, *Thomas Edison: Professional Inventor* (London, 1976); W. Bernard Carlson and A.J. Millard, "Edison as a Manager of Innovations: Lessons for Today," *New Jersey Bell Journal* 8 (Winter, 1985–86): 24–32; Reese V. Jenkins, "Elements of Style: Continuities in Edison's Thinking," *Annals of the New York Academy of Sciences* 424 (1984): 149–62; Jenkins, "Words, Images, Artifacts and Sound: Documents for the History of Technology," *BJHS* 20 (1987): 39–56; David A. Hounshell, "Edison and the Pure Science Ideal in 19th-century America," *Science* 207 (February 8, 1980): 612–17. See also E.A. Norwig, "The Patents of Thomas A. Edison," *Journal of the Patent Office Society* 36 (March, 1954): 213–14; A. Michael McMahon, *The Making of a Profession: A Century of*

Electrical Engineering in America (New York, 1984). Israel Rubin, ed., "Thomas Alva Edison's 'Treatise on National Economic Policy and Business,'" *Business History Review* 59 (Autumn, 1985): 433–64, helps to explain Edison's business values.

An important topic in recent scholarship is the institutionalization of research and development and the evolution of industrial research. Edison's Menlo Park and West Orange facilities figure prominently in these discussions and are the subject of two new studies: William S. Pretzer, ed., *Working at Inventing: Thomas Edison and the Menlo Park Experience* (Dearborn, 1989), is an anthology dealing with a range of topics from telegraphy and telephony to machine shop culture. A.J. Millard's *Edison and the Business of Innovation* (Baltimore, 1990), fills a gap in our understanding of the myriad inventive, testing, and manufacturing activities conducted at "the best lab ever." It also delves into the establishment of Thomas A. Edison, Inc., and Edison's participation on the Naval Consulting Board. See also Byron M. Vanderbilt, "America's First R & D Center," *Industrial Research* 18 (November 15, 1976): 27–31; and David W. Hutchings, *Edison at Work: The Thomas A. Edison Laboratory at West Orange, New Jersey* (New York, 1969). Byron M. Vanderbilt's *Thomas Edison, Chemist* (Washington, D.C., 1971), discusses chemical research essential to several key inventions.

For more general discussion on industrial research during the years of Edison's life, see Leonard S. Reich, *The Making of American Industrial Research: Science and Business at GE and Bell, 1876–1926* (Cambridge, Mass., 1985); George Wise, *Willis R. Whitney, General Electric, and the Origins of U.S. Industrial Research* (New York, 1985); David E. Nye, *Image Worlds: Corporate Identities at General Electric, 1890–1930* (Cambridge, Mass., 1985); and A. Oleson and J. Voss, eds., *The Organization of Research in Modern America* (Baltimore, 1979). See also Reich, "Edison, Coolidge and Langmuir," *Journal of Economic History* 47 (June, 1987): 341–51.

On the more specific issue of the naval research laboratory in World War I, see Lloyd N. Scott, *Naval Consulting Board of the United States* (Washington, D.C., 1920); David K. Allison, "The Origins of the Naval Research Laboratory," *Proceedings of the*

U.S. Naval Institute (July, 1979): 62–69; Theodore A. Thelander, "Josephus Daniels and the Publicity Campaign for Naval and Industrial Preparedness Before World War I," *North Carolina Historical Review* 43 (July, 1966): 316–32; and Thomas P. Hughes, *Elmer Sperry: Inventor and Engineer* (Baltimore, 1971).

For the best discussion of the revolution in business organization, see Alfred P. Chandler, Jr., *The Visible Hand: The Managerial Revolution in American Business* (Cambridge, Mass., 1977). On manufacturing techniques, see David Hounshell, *From the American System to Mass Production, 1800–1932* (Baltimore, 1984).

The inventions associated with Edison span the history of American technology for several decades. There has been a recent explosion in research on the impact of urban telegraphy. Paul B. Israel has been conducting important research on corporate strategy in the telegraph industry, and, with Robert Rosenberg, the development of intra-urban telegraphy. See Paul B. Israel, "From the Machine Shop to the Industrial Laboratory: Telegraphy and the Changing Context of American Invention, 1830–1920" (PhD Dissertation, Rutgers University, 1989). See also Joel A. Tarr, with Thomas Finholt and David Goodman, "The City and the Telegraph: Urban Telecommunications in the Pre-Telephone Era," *Journal of Urban History* 14 (November, 1987): 38–80; Richard DuBoff, "Business Demand and the Development of the Telegraph in the United States, 1844–1860," *Business History Review* 54 (Winter, 1980): 459–79; Keith A. Nier and Andrew J. Butrica, "Telegraphy Becomes a World System," *Essays in Economic and Business History* 6 (1988): 211–16, and research by Nier on the quadruplex. For an older general account on the telegraph, see Robert Luther Thompson, *Wiring a Continent: The History of the Telegraph Industry in the United States, 1832–1866* (Princeton, 1947).

While very little new work has been devoted to Edison's role in the development of the telephone, Johns Hopkins Press has published several key business histories on the telephone industry in its AT&T Series in Telephone History: Robert W. Garnet, *The Telephone Enterprise: The Evolution of the Bell's System's Horizontal Structure, 1876–1909* (Baltimore, 1985); Kenneth Lipartito, *The Bell System and Regional Business: The Telephone in the South, 1877–1920* (Baltimore, 1989); George David Smith, *The Anatomy of a Business Strategy: Bell, Western Electric and the Origins of the American Telephone Industry* (Baltimore, 1985); Neil Wasserman, *From Invention to Innovation: Long-Distance Telephone Transmission at the Turn of the Century* (Baltimore, 1985). See also Carolyn Marvin, *When Old Technologies Were New: Thinking About Electric Communication in the Late Nineteenth Century* (New York, 1988), and Robert V. Bruce, *Alexander Graham Bell and the Conquest of Solitude* (Boston, 1973).

As might be expected, the electric light and power systems have been a central focus of research. Robert Freidel and Paul Israel, *Edison's Electric Light: Biography of an Invention* (New Brunswick, New Jersey, 1986), is the most thorough treatment of the electric light and the process of invention. Thomas P. Hughes, "The Electrification of America: The System Builders," *Technology and Culture* 20 (January, 1979): 124–61, and *Networks of Power: Electrification in Western Society, 1880–1930* (Baltimore, 1983), treat Edison's role as a system builder and the proliferation of the lighting system. See also National Museum of History and Technology, *Edison: Lighting a Revolution; The Beginning of Electric Power,* Bernard S. Finn, curator (Washington, D.C., 1979); George Wise, "Swan's Way: A Study in Style," *IEEE Spectrum* 19 (April, 1982): 66–70; Christopher S. Derganc, "Thomas Edison and His Electric Lighting System," *IEEE Spectrum* 16 (February, 1979): 50–59; Charles Wrege and Ronald G. Greenwood, "The War Against Isolated Plants by Central Stations, 1901–1918," *Essays in Economic and Business History* 6 (1988): 189–99; Robert Conot, "Twin of a Feeble Edison 1879 Light Bulb Casts One-candle Power Glow for Centenary," *Smithsonian* 10 (July, 1979): 34–43; Richard Rudolph, "Set Right the History of Electric Power: Charles Brush Credited, Edison's Role Corrected, Public Systems Led the Way," *Public Power* (September–October, 1987): 30–39; and Philip McGuire, "Technology and Commerce: The Gas Light Industry's Response to Edison's Electric Bulb," *Potomac Review* 6 (1973): 70–75. See also Warren D. Devine, Jr., "From Shafts to Wires: Historical Perspective on Electrification," *Journal of Economic History* 43 (1983):

347–72. On the origins of Edison's interest in the electric light, see Philip J. Roberts, "Edison, the Electric Light and the Eclipse," *Annals of Wyoming* 53 (1981): 54–62, and Eric N. Moody, "Tom Edison and the Bonanzagraph," *Nevada Historical Society Quarterly* 27 (Fall, 1984): 199–206.

"The battle of the currents" has attracted substantial attention. See Thomas P. Hughes, "Harold P. Brown and the Executioner's Current: An Incident in the AC-DC Controversy," *Business History Review* 32 (Summer, 1958): 143–65; Terry S. Reynolds and Theodore Bernstein, "The Damnable Alternating Current," *Proceedings of the IEEE* 64 (September, 1976): 1339–43; Philip L. Alger and Robert E. Arnold, "The History of Induction Motors in America," *Proceedings of the IEEE* 64 (September, 1976): 1380–83; Paul A. David and Julie Ann Bunn, "The Economics of Gateway Technologies and Network Evolution: Lessons from Electricity Supply History," *Information Economics and Policy* (forthcoming); David and Bunn, "'The Battle of the Systems' and the Evolutionary Dynamics of Network Technology Rivalries," High Technology Impact Program, Working Paper no. 15 (Center for Economic Policy Research, Stanford University, 1987); Paul A. David, "The Hero and the Herd in Technological History: Reflections on Thomas Edison and the 'Battle of the Systems,'" Center for Economic Policy, Research Publication no. 100 (Stanford University, 1987); and W. Bernard Carlson and A.J. Millard, "Defining Risk in a Business Context: Thomas A. Edison and Elihu Thomson, and the a.c.-d.c. controversy, 1885–1900," in B.B. Johnson and V.T. Covello, eds., *The Social Cultural Construction of Risk* (Dordrecht, Holland, 1987).

For general treatments of Edison and the power industry, see Hughes, *Networks of Power*; James E. Brittain, "The International Diffusion of Electrical Power Technology, 1870–1920, *Journal of Economic History* 34 (March, 1974): 108–21; Brian Bowers, *A History of Electric Light and Power* (London, 1982); Arthur A. Bright, Jr., *The Electric-Lamp Industry* (New York, 1972; orig., 1949); Harold I. Sharlin, *The Making of the Electrical Age* (London, 1963); Robert Silverberg, *Light for the World: Edison and the Power Industry* (Princeton, New Jersey, 1967); Harold C. Passer, *The*

Electrical Manufacturers, 1875–1900 (New York, 1972); and Martin V. Melosi, *Coping with Abundance: Energy and Environment in Industrial America* (New York, 1985).

Historical research on other important Edison inventions pale by comparison with the electric light. Millard's study of West Orange provides one of the best treatments of the Edison phonograph. See also Oliver Read and Walter L. Welch, *From Tin Foil to Stereo: Evolution of the Phonograph* (Indianapolis, 1959); Jay K. Lucker, "Phonograph Is Now Perfect," *Princeton University Library Chronicle* 25 (Spring, 1964): 220–25; and Roland Gelatt, *The Fabulous Phonograph: From Edison to Stereo* (New York, 1965; rev. ed.).

On the storage battery, see Richard Schallenberg, "The Alkaline Storage Battery: A Case Study in the Edisonian Method," *Synthesis* 1 (Winter, 1972): 3–13; Schallenberg, "The Anomalous Storage Battery: An American Lag in Early Electrical Engineering," *Technology and Culture* 22 (1981): 725–52; Schallenberg, *Bottle Energy: Electrical Engineering and the Evolution of Chemical Energy Storage* (Philadelphia, 1982); and W.H. Meadowcroft, *Edison and His Storage Battery* (Orange, New Jersey, 1928).

On the ore-milling operation, see W. Barnard Carlson, "Edison in the Mountains: The Magnetic Ore Separation Venture, 1879–1900," in Norman Smith, ed., *History of Technology* (London and New York, 1983): 37–59; George S. May and Victor F. Lemmer, "Thomas Edison's Experimental Work with Michigan Iron Ore," *Michigan History* 53 (Summer, 1969): 109–30; John D. Venable, "Big Rocks and Rocky Years," *New Jersey History* 99 (Spring–Summer, 1981): 81–101; and Thomas W. Leidy and Donald R. Shenton, "Titan in Berks: Edison's Experiments in Iron Concentration," *Historical Review of Berks County* 23 (Fall, 1958): 104–10.

On the tasimeter, see John A. Eddy, "Thomas A. Edison and Infra-red Astronomy," *Journal of the History of Astronomy* 3 (1972): 165–87. See also David A. E. Shepherd, "The Contributions of Alexander Graham Bell and Thomas Alva Edison to

Medicine," *Bulletin of the History of Medicine* 51 (1977): 610–16; Harold G. Bowen, *The Edison Effect* (West Orange, New Jersey, 1951); and Harriet Sprague, *Frank J. Sprague and the Edison Myth* (New York, 1947).

The controversial role of Edison and the commercialization of motion pictures has led to a flurry of studies focusing either on Edison's part in the invention of motion pictures or his influence in establishing a monopoly in the field. Gordon Hendricks, a staunch advocate of W.K.L. Dickson, leveled a harsh criticism of Edison in *Edison Motion Picture Myth* (Berkeley, Calif., 1961); *The Kinetoscope: America's First Commercially Successful Motion Picture Exhibitor* (New York, 1966); and *The Beginnings of the Biograph* (New York, 1964). Others have picked up on Hendrick's criticism, particularly Robert Sklar, *Movie-Made America: A Cultural History of American Movies* (New York, 1974). On the MPPC and monopoly, see Robert Anderson, "The Motion Picture Patents Company: A Reevaluation," in Tino Balio, ed., *The American Film Industry* (Madison, Wisconsin, 1985; rev. ed.): 133–52; Ralph Cassady, Jr., "Monopoly in Motion Picture Production and Distribution: 1908–1915," *Southern California Law Review* 32 (Summer, 1959): 325–90; and Jeanne Thomas Allen, "The Decay of the Motion Picture Patents Company," *Cinema Journal* 10 (Spring, 1971): 34–40. See also John F. Fell, ed., *Film Before Griffith* (Berkeley, Calif., 1983); Anthony Slide, *The Big V: A History of the Vitagraph Company* (1976); Jon Gartenberg, "Camera Movement in Edison and Biograph Films, 1900–1906," *Cinema Journal* 19 (Spring, 1980): 1–16; and Garth Jowett, *Film: The Democratic Art* (Boston, 1976).

During the latter years of Edison's life, his role as a celebrity overcame his creative activity. Wachhorst's *Thomas Alva Edison* handles the subject very well. Edison's key relationship with Henry Ford, however, has only been treated in brief episodes in the Edison literature and in the vast list of Ford biographies. For example, see Robert Lacey, *Ford: The Men and the Machine* (Boston, 1986); William Adams Simonds, *Henry Ford and Greenfield Village* (New York, 1938); Allan Nevins, *Henry Ford* 3 vols. (New

York, 1954–1963); Keith Sward, *The Legend of Henry Ford* (New York, 1948); Albert Lee, *Henry Ford and the Jews* (New York, 1980); William C. Richards, *The Last Billionaire* (New York, 1948); David L. Lewis, *The Public Image of Henry Ford* (Detroit, 1976); and Barbara S. Kraft, *The Peace Ship* (New York, 1978).

Acknowledgments

This book was made much easier by the help of several colleagues, archivists, and benefactors. The financial support of the New Jersey Historical Commission was central. I was able to conduct research in West Orange, New Jersey; Washington, D.C.; and Dearborn, Michigan, because of the commission's generosity. The Energy Laboratory at the University of Houston, under the direction of Alvin Hildebrandt, provided much appreciated supplemental support, as did the Limited-Grant-In-Aid committee at the University.

Because new scholarship on Thomas Edison kept pouring out regularly, I had to depend on colleagues with unpublished articles and books for the latest information and interpretations. Paul Israel, Andre Millard, and Joel Tarr were kind enough to share their important work and to critique the manuscript. I also appreciated the guidance and advice of other colleagues, including Melodie Andrews, Bernard Carlson, James Jones, John Lenihan, Keith Nier, John O'Connor, Joseph Pratt, William Pretzer, and Mark Rose. Special thanks to Oscar Handlin for his superb editing.

I am also grateful to the staffs of the various depositories I visited, especially Mimi Bowling, former archivist at the Edison Archives in West Orange; Edward Pershey, former curator at the Edison Historic Site; Judith Endelman, librarian at the Henry Ford Museum; and Reese Jenkins's Edison Papers staff.

And finally, much love to my wife, Carolyn, and daughters, Gina and Adria, for putting up with their preoccupied—and often grumpy—husband and father.

Martin V. Melosi

Index